T0303986

ROUTLEDGE LIBRARY EDITIONS:
TAXATION

Volume 7

THE MACROECONOMIC EFFECTS OF WAR FINANCE IN THE UNITED STATES

THE MACROECONOMIC EFFECTS OF WAR FINANCE IN THE UNITED STATES

Taxes, Inflation, and Deficit Finance

LEE E. OHANIAN

Routledge
Taylor & Francis Group

LONDON AND NEW YORK

First published in 1998 by Garland Publishing, Inc.

This edition first published in 2019
by Routledge
2 Park Square, Milton Park, Abingdon, Oxon OX14 4RN

and by Routledge
711 Third Avenue, New York, NY 10017

Routledge is an imprint of the Taylor & Francis Group, an informa business

© 1998 Lee E. Ohanian

British Library Cataloguing in Publication Data
A catalogue record for this book is available from the British Library

ISBN: 978-1-138-56291-2 (Set)
ISBN: 978-0-429-48988-4 (Set) (ebk)
ISBN: 978-0-8153-4966-2 (Volume 7) (hbk)
ISBN: 978-1-351-10887-4 (Volume 7) (ebk)

Publisher's Note
The publisher has gone to great lengths to ensure the quality of this reprint but points out that some imperfections in the original copies may be apparent.

Disclaimer
The publisher has made every effort to trace copyright holders and would welcome correspondence from those they have been unable to trace.

THE MACROECONOMIC EFFECTS OF WAR FINANCE IN THE UNITED STATES

TAXES, INFLATION, AND DEFICIT FINANCE

LEE E. OHANIAN

GARLAND PUBLISHING, INC.
A MEMBER OF THE TAYLOR & FRANCIS GROUP
NEW YORK & LONDON / 1998

Library of Congress Cataloging-in-Publication Data

Ohanian, Lee E.
  The macroeconomic effects of war finance in the United
States : taxes, inflation, and deficit finance.
      p.   cm. — (Financial sector of the American economy)
  Includes bibliographical references and index.
  ISBN 0-8153-3040-5 (alk. paper)
  1. Finance, Public—United States—History. 2. World War,
1939–1945—Finance—United States. 3. Korean War, 1950–
1953—Finance—United States. 4. Monetary policy—United
States—History. I. Title. II. Series.
HJ257.038 1998
336.73—dc21

                                                  98-39521

Printed on acid-free, 250-year-life paper
Manufactured in the United States of America

Dedication

For Andrew and Sarah–

you are the greatest kids a Dad could ever hope for.

Contents

List of Tables

List of Illustrations

Acknowledgments

This book has benefited greatly from the comments of Robert King, Alan Stockman, Stan Engerman and my advisor, Thomas Cooley. I also thank Ron Edwards and Dan Houser for their excellent research assistance, and Paul Drapiewski for his expertise and patience in transforming my dissertation into this book.

The Macroeconomic
Effects of War Finance
in the United States

I

Introduction

This book presents a quantitative investigation of the macroeconomic effects of different fiscal and monetary policies that have been used to finance wars in the U.S. I examine both positive and normative effects of historical government policies.

Most wars in the U.S. have been financed primarily with nominal (dollar denominated) government debt and money creation, rather than with contemporaneous distorting taxes. While distorting taxes rose somewhat during U.S. war episodes, the extra revenue from higher taxes typically fell far short of government spending requirements. An important exception to this characterization occurred during the Korean War. Money creation was very low during this conflict, and very little debt was issued. Instead, higher taxes on factor incomes generated sufficient revenue to satisfy government demand. President Truman was well known to be a strong advocate of balanced budget financing. Studenski and Kroos (1963) note that Truman hoped to maintain a balanced budget even if military costs doubled during the Korean War, and report Truman as stating "The American people understand that if we had paid higher taxes in World War II, we would be better off today."

In Chapter 2, I investigate some of the implications of President Truman's arguments. To accomplish this, I use a dynamic general equilibrium model with capital and labor income taxes. In particular, I analyze the effects of financing World War II with a high-tax policy similar to that used during the Korean War. I also analyze the effects of financing the Korean War with a tax-smoothing policy similar to that used during World War II. I find that a high-tax policy would have resulted in sharply lower labor supply, capital, and output relative to the actual policy used. In particular, I calculate that the welfare cost of World War II would have doubled had the Korean-type policy been used, as advocated by President Truman. I also find that a modest welfare benefit would have resulted from the use of a tax-smoothing policy during the Korean War.

In Chapter 3, I analyze some issues associated with the conduct of wartime monetary policy. While it was common to print money during wars to help finance the war effort, it was also common to pursue a deflationary policy after the war ended and return the price level to its prewar value. The money supply doubled over the course of World War II, but instead of conducting deflationary policy after the war, the money supply continued to grow, and the price level rose about 60 percent. One result of this unexpected inflation was to reduce the real value of the outstanding public debt.

I introduce money into the model economy via a cash-in-advance constraint, and conduct a counterfactual exercise in which the government does pursue a deflationary policy after the war and fully honors government debt by raising taxes on factor incomes. I find that the welfare gain from the surprise inflation was equivalent to about three percent of consumption in perpetuity. In addition, I estimate that the capital stock today is about $1 trillion higher than it would be had the deflationary policy been used.

A second important aspect of World War II monetary policy was the imposition of price controls. General price controls were in place by April 1942, and continued over the course of the war. I analyze the effects of the controls by modifying the model to account for maximum legal prices, rationing, and "black market" activity. Within this model, the imposition of controls results in lower labor supply, consumption, output, and capital. Given the controls in place during the war, the observed sharp increase in labor supply that occurred is somewhat difficult to account for.

II

The Macroeconomic Effects of Wartime Fiscal Policy in the United States

2.1 INTRODUCTION

Since organized societies have waged war, policy makers and economists have struggled with the problem of how best to finance war expenditures. Alexander Hamilton (1787), for example, recognized the benefit of issuing debt to finance emergency government spending, but also maintained that war debts should be honored, even if it meant significantly higher postwar taxes. [For a summary of Hamilton's positions, see Lucas (1981).] Keynes (1940) was deeply concerned with the potential resource demands of Britain's efforts in World War II, and constructed a detailed policy to finance temporary war expenditures. The "radical" Keynes plan, submitted to the Chancellor of the Exchequer, included the use of rationing and price controls, a sharply progressive surtax on private incomes, and a capital levy following the war. It is clear from these proposals that an important element of the Keynes policy was to generate significant revenue from contemporaneous taxation of factor incomes, in addition to shifting as much of the financial burden of the war as possible to wealthy citizens.

Academic interest in this area was revived by Barro (1979), and Lucas and Stokey (1983), who considered the following question: Given that governments must finance exogenous expenditures with distorting taxes, what set of tax, monetary, and debt policies minimize the deadweight loss of taxation?[1] The focus of Barro, Lucas and Stokey, and much of the other literature on optimal taxation has been to analyze the efficient financing of large, temporary government spending shocks, such as war expenditures. One conclusion that emerges from this research program is the principle of tax smoothing; tax rates should not necessarily adjust to public finance shocks such that a balanced budget is always achieved. Rather, sure government debt, as in Barro (1979), or Arrow-Debreu contingent claims, as in Lucas and Stokey (1983), absorb excess government spending requirements. The debt issue in Barro's analysis makes it possible to spread tax distortions over time, while the state contingent insurance of Lucas and Stokey enables spending shocks to be financed by non-distorting transfers from consumers to the government.

Many war episodes in the United States, as well as those of other developed countries, exhibit certain characteristics that appear to be consistent with some predictions of optimal tax models. During World War II, for example, U.S. war expenditures were financed partially by issuing debt that ultimately yielded large, negative real returns to bond holders. A similar pattern of fiscal and monetary policy is evident during the Revolutionary War, the War of 1812, the Civil War, World War I, and to a lesser extent, the Vietnam War. Government policy, however, was strikingly different during the Korean War. Expenditures were financed almost exclusively by higher capital and labor income taxes. Inflation was very low during this period, and for much of the Korean War, the Federal government recorded budget surpluses, rather than deficits.

The purpose of this paper is to evaluate quantitatively the economic effects of the different government policies used to finance these two U.S. wars. Both positive and normative issues are examined. In particular, I analyze the welfare costs associated with these different policies, and also study their effect on aggregate variables such as output and the capital stock. A general equilibrium model with capital and labor income taxes is used in this study, and welfare costs are analyzed using the approach of Cooley and Hansen (1990).Taking expenditures of specific war episodes as exogenous, the model economy is first used to estimate the effects of the actual government policies that were in place during these periods. The consequences of financing wars with different fiscal policies is also analyzed. Given the substantial policy differences between World War II and the Korean War, counterfactual experiments are used to explore the implications of financing World War II like the Korean War, and similarly, financing the Korean War like World War II. I conclude from these experiments that historical differences in wartime government policies have important positive and normative implications.

Section 2.2 provides a brief overview of these war episodes, highlighting differences in economic policy across war periods. Section 2.3 describes the model economy used in this paper, and summarizes the method used to approximate the competitive equilibrium. Section 2.4 discusses model calibration, and the technique of examining welfare costs in these economies. Section 2.5 presents the welfare calculations and analyzes other economic effects for different experiments in war financing. A summary and conclusion are presented in 2.6.

2.2 HISTORICAL WAR EPISODES

The emphasis in this chapter is to analyze the economic effects of different government policies for war financing. Perhaps the most significant difference between the fiscal policies used to finance U.S. wars were those of World War II and the Korean War. This section summarizes the behavior of the U.S. economy during these two wars, and in particular, highlights differences in monetary and fiscal policy across the two periods.

Growth in real output was considerable during both wars. Real GNP advanced 62 percent between 1940 and 1945, which represents an average annual growth rate of 10.1 percent. Compared to the natural rate series of output constructed by Balke and Gordon (1986), GNP was 27 percent above trend at the peak of the war in 1944.

Real output grew at a 5.8 percent annual rate during the Korean War, rising from nearly four percent below trend just prior to the war, to 5.5 percent above the Balke-Gordon natural rate index in 1952. The growth in output during these two war episodes can be primarily accounted for by increased labor supply and higher total factor productivity. Consumer spending rose during both wars, but at less than the long-term growth rate. The capital stock declined during World War II, but advanced significantly over the course of the Korean War.

The considerable increase in output during World War II reflected the enormous rise in military spending.[2] At the peak of the war, government spending absorbed over 40 percent of GNP. Korean War spending was more moderate, with government spending accounting for a maximum of about 20 percent of GNP.

It is common to associate war episodes with high inflation [see Goldin (1980)]. Row 2 of Table 1 displays the behavior of aggregate prices during four major wars in the history of the U.S. Inflation during the Korean War stands in sharp contrast to inflation in all other war periods. Wholesale prices between 1951 and 1953 rose just two percent, compared to an increase of 108 percent during World War II.

Friedman and Schwarz (1963) attribute the striking difference in inflation performance during the Korean War to monetary policy. Rows 3 and 4 of Table 1 present data on the money stock during World War II and the Korean War. Money growth was very rapid and volatile during World War II. The average growth rate of M1, which consists primarily of currency and demand deposits, between 1940 and 1946 was 18 percent, with a maximum increase of 30 percent in 1943. The standard deviation of money growth was 2.5 percent. During the Korean War, M1 grew very slowly, with an average rate increase of just four percent. Maximum growth occurred in 1952, with an increase of only 4.9 percent.

It is important to emphasize not only the slow growth of M1 during the Korean War, but also the lack of variability in the money stock. The standard deviation of M1 growth was just 0.3 percent, which is nearly one tenth as large as money growth volatility in world War II, and 80 percent smaller than the World War I experience. In fact, Friedman and Schwartz (1963) found that the volatility of money growth during the Korean War was the lowest in the post-civil war history of the United States. This statistic provides important evidence of a policy shift separating the Korean War from other U.S. war episodes.

Table 1
Descriptive Statistics---Selected U.S. Wars

	Korea (1950-53)	WW II (1941-46)	WWI (1917-18)	Civil War (1861-64)
Output Growth	5.8%	10.1%	15.5%	NA
Inflation Rate (W.P.I.)	0.4%	9.6%	14.6%	29.5%
Money Growth (M1)	4.0%	18.0%	11.1%	NA
Standard Dev. Money Growth	0.3%	2.5%	5.4%	NA
Govt. Spending Dev. from Trend	29.0%	124.0%	91.0%	NA
Ave. Cap. Taxes: During war	62.6%	60.2%	NA	NA
Ave. Cap. Taxes: Prior to War	49.9%	45.1%	NA	NA
Ave. Labor Taxes: During War	19.8%	17.5%	NA	NA
Ave. Labor Taxes: Prior to War	16.2%	9.1%	NA	NA

Sources: Lines 1–4, Balke and Gordon (1986), and Goldin (1980).
Line 5, Basic Data: Kendrick (1961). Lines 6–9: Joines (1981).

Labor income tax rates, and to a lesser extent, capital tax rates, rose during World War II. Prior to World War II, the average marginal tax rate on capital was about 45 percent, and the average marginal labor tax rate was just nine percent. During World War II, labor tax rates rose to about 19 percent, and capital tax rates averaged about 60 percent. While these higher tax rates generated significant revenues, they were not nearly sufficient to finance war spending. The U.S. government issued considerable debt during the war at nominal interest rates ranging between .375 and 2.5 percent. The debt-GNP ratio at the end of the war was a record 1.3. The ex-post real rate of return on government debt averaged -5.2 percent during World War II [see Barro (1984), p.315]. After the war, labor tax rates fell slightly to 16 percent, and capital tax rates fell to 49 percent.

Taxes rose again during the Korean War, with capital tax rates rising to an average of nearly 63 percent. This represents the highest rate of capital income taxation in the history of the U.S. [see Joines (1981)]. Labor tax rates rose from 16 percent to just under 20 percent. It is important to note that the extra revenue generated by these tax increases was sufficient to finance the Korean War effort. The average tax rates during the two wars are presented in rows 6 and 8 of Table 1. During the Korean War, the federal government did not rely on deficit financing. The market value of the national debt, which was $1.5 billion just prior to the start of the war in 1949, stood at $1.47 billion in 1952 [See Seater (1982, 1985)].

Perhaps the most striking indicator of the difference in monetary and fiscal policy in U.S. wars can be seen in Table 2, which is taken from Goldin (1980). These data show that the U.S. has typically financed wars using a mix of direct

Table 2

War Financing in the United States

Estimated Percentage of Expenditures Financed by:

	Direct Taxes	Debt and Seignorage
Revolutionary War	13.1	86.9
War of 1812	21.0	79.0
Mexican War	41.8	58.2
Civil War Union	9.3	90.7
Civil War Confederacy	13.0	87.0
Spanish-American War	66.0	34.0
World War I	24.0	76.0
World War II	41.0	59.0
Korean War	100.0	0.0

Source: Goldin (1980), pp. 938-940.

contemporaneous taxes, debt and money creation. In particular, 24% of war expenditures were financed via direct taxes, on average, across the two world wars and the Civil War, with the balance financed by debt and money creation. During the Korean War, virtually all war expenditures were financed by contemporaneous distorting taxes.

These data clearly illustrate the significant differences in economic policy that accompanied World War II and the Korean War. Korean War expenditures were financed almost exclusively by contemporaneously higher distorting taxes, in particular, higher capital income taxes. Very little government debt was issued, and inflation was remarkably low and stable, even by peacetime standards.

This policy mix was not arrived at by accident; Studenski and Kroos (1963) report that president Truman continuously urged Congress "to finance the greatest possible amount by taxation," and that he "hoped to maintain a balanced budget, even if military costs doubled" (page 490). With an emphasis on balanced budgets, tight money, and high taxes, macroeconomic policy during the Korean War seems reminiscent of the sharply criticized policies pursued by the Hoover Administration and the Federal Reserve at the start of the Great Depression. Korean War policy clearly did not provide for any meaningful smoothing of tax of distortions. In sharp contrast, government policies during World War II allowed for apparently significant smoothing. The U.S. Treasury floated substantial nominal debt during the war that yielded negative ex-post real rates of return. The low yields on these securities partially reflected very high and variable rates of inflation. The differences in war financing during these two episodes represent an important regime shift in the history of U.S. economic policy.

2.3 THE MODEL ECONOMY

In this section, I use a dynamic general equilibrium model that includes capital and labor income taxation to evaluate the economic effects of the different wartime fiscal policies pursued during World War II and the Korean War. This strategy provides a tractable way to obtain quantitative estimates of the welfare costs of different policies, and analyze the effects of these policies on aggregate variables such as output and the capital stock. This approach is also widely used in macroeconomics and public finance.

The economy consists of a continuum of identical, infinitely-lived households on the unit interval endowed initially with k units of capital, and one unit of time each period. Consumers receive income from labor and capital services, matured government debt, and government transfers, and use income to purchase consumption goods, finance new investment, and purchase government bonds. Output is produced from a stochastic, constant returns to scale technology by a competitive firm using capital and labor. The government faces an exogenously given stochastic sequence of spending requirements that are financed by taxing labor and capital income, and issuing debt. I assume that lump sum taxes are not available.

The representative household in this economy maximizes the following lifetime utility function:

$$(2.1) \qquad \text{Max } E \sum_{t=0}^{\infty} \beta^t (\log(c_t) - \gamma n_t) \qquad 0 < \beta < 1.$$

c_t is consumption and n_t is the fraction of time spent working, while β is the household's subjective discount factor.

Following Hansen (1985), hours worked for the representative household enters utility linearly. This specification, which follows from Rogerson's (1988) indivisible labor assumption with lotteries, allows the model economy to exhibit significant fluctuations in labor input in response to shocks to productivity and government spending.[3]

Consumers maximize (2.1) subject to the following sequence of wealth constraints:

$$TR_t + (1 + R_t)b_t + (1 - \delta)k_t + (1 - \tau_{kt})r_t k_t + \tau_{kt}\delta k_t +$$

(2.2)
$$(1 - \tau_{nt})w_t n_t \geq k_{t+1} + b_{t+1} + c_t.$$

Each period, households purchase consumption (c_t) and new government debt (b_{t+1}), and carry forward next period's capital stock (k_{t+1}). Funding for these purchases includes after-tax labor income $(1 - \tau_{nt})w_t n_t$ and capital income $(1 - \tau_{kt})r_t k_t$, where w_t is the real wage, and r_t is the real rental rate of capital, transfers from the government (TR_t), and principal and interest on matured government debt $[(1 + R_t)b_t]$. The term $\tau_{kt}\delta k_t$ is included to capture the depreciation allowance in the tax code.

Household investment is defined as:[4]

(2.3)
$$x_t = k_{t+1} - (1 - \delta)k_t$$

A competitive firm produces output from the Cobb-Douglas production function:

(2.4)
$$Y_t = \lambda_t K_t^{\theta} N_t^{1-\theta}, \qquad 0 < \theta < 1$$

Capital letters indicate per capita quantities, which competitive households view parametrically. In rational expectations equilibrium, household choices will equal per capita quantities.

λ_t, which is the technology shock, evolves exogenously according to the law of motion:

$$
\begin{aligned}
\log(\lambda_t) &= \rho_\lambda \log(\lambda_{t-1}) + \epsilon_{\lambda t}, \\
0 &< \rho_\lambda < 1, \quad E(\epsilon_\lambda) = 0, \quad E(\epsilon_\lambda^2) = \sigma_{\epsilon\lambda}^2.
\end{aligned}
$$

(2.5)

Given constant returns to scale, profit maximization by the firm will yield zero economic profits, and implies the following functions for wage and rental rates:

(2.6) $\qquad w(K_t, N_t, \lambda_t) = \lambda_t (1 - \theta) [K_t / N_t]^\theta$

(2.7) $\qquad r(K_t, N_t, \lambda_t) = \lambda_t \theta [N_t / K_t]^{1-\theta}.$

Government exists to finance a non-negative sequence of required expenditures $\{g_t\}_{t=0}^\infty$. Following Lucas and Stokey (1983), I assume that government expenditures do not enter utility functions or enhance private sector productivity.[5] Government spending is satisfied by capital and labor tax revenues, and by issuing real one-period debt. The law of motion for government spending is:

$$\log(g_t) = v_{gt}(\Psi) + u_{gt}, \quad u_{gt} = \rho_g u_{gt-1} + \epsilon_{gt},$$

(2.8)

$$E(\epsilon_{gt}^2) = \sigma_{\epsilon gt}^2(\Psi)$$

Capital and labor income tax rates ($\{\tau_{kt}(\Psi)\}_{t=0}^{\infty}$ and $\{\tau_{nt}(\Psi)\}_{t=0}^{\infty}$) and the parameters describing the government spending process ($v_{gt}(\Psi), \sigma_{\epsilon gt}^2(\Psi)$) are assumed to be functions of the war/peace state $\psi_i \in \Psi$. The states are chosen to approximate an economy which is initially in peace, but faces the possibility of fighting World War II. Following World War II, the economy faces the possibility of fighting the Korean War, followed by peace. There are four transient states, and a fifth state (post-Korean War peace) which is the only ergodic set. The states are:

ψ_1: Prewar peace (pre-World War II)

ψ_2: World War II

ψ_3: Interwar (post-World War II, pre-Korean War)

ψ_4: Korean War

ψ_5: Postwar peace

I assume the following Markov processes for the transition probabilities for the war/peace states:

(2.9a) $$\Pr(\psi_{t+1} = \psi_1 | \psi_t = \psi_1) = P_1$$

(2.9b) $$\Pr(\psi_{t+1} = \psi_2 | \psi_t = \psi_1) = (1 - P_1)$$

(2.10a) $$\Pr(\psi_{t+1} = \psi_2 | \psi_t = \psi_2) = P_{2t} =$$
$$P_2 \text{(duration of World War II)}$$

(2.10b) $$\Pr(\psi_{t+1} = \psi_3 | \psi_t = \psi_2) = (1 - P_{2t})$$

(2.11a) $$\Pr(\psi_{t+1} = \psi_3 | \psi_t = \psi_3) = P_3$$

(2.11b) $$\Pr(\psi_{t+1} = \psi_4 | \psi_t = \psi_3) = (1 - P_3)$$

(2.12a) $$\Pr(\psi_{t+1} = \psi_4 | \psi_t = \psi_4) = P_{4t} =$$
$$P_4 \text{(duration of Korean War)}$$

(2.12b) $$\Pr(\psi_{t+1} = \psi_5 | \psi_t = \psi_4) = (1 - P_{4t})$$

(2.13) $$\Pr(\psi_{t+1} = \psi_5 | \psi_t = \psi_5) = 1$$

Assuming that post-Korean War peace is an absorbing state allows me to isolate the effects of World War II and the Korean War, and facilitates the welfare calculations presented in Section 2.5.

I assume that there is a constant probability, $1 - P_1$, of the outbreak of World War II. This simplifies the solution procedure, and avoids the difficult task of trying to identify historical expectations of the outbreak of the war. Once in World War II, the probability of remaining in the state is assumed to be a time-invariant function of the current duration of the war, P_2(duration). Following the end of war, there is a constant probability $1 - P_3$ of the outbreak of the

Korean War. As in the case of the World War II state, once the Korean War has been realized, the probability of remaining in the war is a time-invariant function of the duration of the war. Following the Korean War, there is peace with probability one. The exact nature and justification of the transition probabilities, and the mapping from the states to the government spending and capital and labor income tax processes, is discussed in Section 4.

I define a balanced budget government policy as one in which for all possible histories, the present value of government expenditures and transfers equals the present value of government revenue:

$$(2.14) \quad \sum_{t=0}^{\infty} \left\{ \left(\prod_{t=0}^{\infty} [1/(1+R_t)] \right) \left[g_t + TR_t - \tau_{nt} w_t N_t - \tau_{kt}(r_t - \delta)K_t \right] \right\} = 0$$

The period government budget constraint requires that spending that is not satisfied by tax revenue is financed by new debt issue:

$$(2.15) \quad \begin{aligned} &G_t + TR_t + (1+R_t)B_t \\ &= \tau_{nt} w_t N_t + \tau_{kt}(r_t - \delta)K_t + B_{t+1} \end{aligned}$$

The aggregate resource constraint for this economy is

$$(2.16) \quad \lambda_t K_t^{\theta} N_t^{1-\theta} \geq C_t + X_t + G_t$$

Given initial endowments of capital, bonds, a balanced budget government policy, and a law of motion for government debt, a competitive equilibrium for this economy consists of sequences for interest rates $\{R_t\}_{t=0}^{\infty}$, factor prices, $\{w_t, r_t\}_{t=0}^{\infty}$, and household allocations, $\{k_{t+1}, b_{t+1}, n_t, c_t\}_{t=0}^{\infty}$, such that:

(1) Given the sequence of interest rates and factor prices, the sequence of allocations maximizes (2.1) subject to the constraints (2.2);

(2) Factor prices satisfy the firm efficiency conditions (2.6) and (2.7);

(3) Interest rates on sure government debt (R_{t+1}) satisfy the pricing relation

$$E_t \left\{ \frac{1}{c_{t+1}} (1 - \tau_{kt+1}) r_{t+1} + (1 - \delta) + \delta \tau_{kt+1} \right\} / E_t \left(\frac{1}{c_{t+1}} \right)$$

$$= 1 + R_{t+1}$$

This restricts government debt to be competitively priced, and implies that households will hold the outstanding stock of government debt in equilibrium

(4) Allocations are feasible, and household choices of bonds, (b_{t+1}), capital, (k_{t+1}), effort, (n_t), and consumption, (c_t), coincide with B_{t+1}, K_{t+1}, N_t, and C_t.

2.3.1 Approximating the Competitive Equilibrium Numerically

Denoting ϕ_t to be the date–t marginal value of wealth, the household's efficiency conditions for this problem are:

(2.17)

(i) $1/c_t = \phi_t$ (consumption)

(ii) $\gamma = \phi_t(1 - \tau_{nt})w_t$ (labor)

(iii) (Capital)

$$\phi_t = \beta E_t\left\{\phi_{t+1}[(1 - \tau_{kt+1})r_{t+1} + (1 - \delta) + \delta\tau_{kt+1}]\right\}$$

(iv) (Government Bond Holdings)

$$\phi_t = \beta E_t[\phi_{t+1}](1 + R_{t+1})$$

(v) (Budget)

$$TR_t + (1 + R_t)b_t + (1 - \delta)k_t + (1 - \tau_{kt})r_t k_t$$

$$+ \tau_{kt}\delta k_t + (1 - \tau_{nt})w_t n_t - k_{t+1} + b_{t+1} + c_t = 0.$$

These first order conditions, with equations 2.4, 2.6, 2.7, 2.15, 2.16, $b_{t+1} = B_{t+1}$, $k_{t+1} = K_{t+1}$, $n_t = N_t$, $c_t = C_t$, and a present value balanced budget policy, characterize the competitive equilibrium of this economy. Since this is a distorted economy, the equilibrium cannot be obtained by solving a social planner's (optimization) problem, as in Kydland and Prescott (1982). There are a number of alternative numerical methods, however, that can be used to approximate the competitive equilibrium.[6]

Given the assumptions regarding the transition probabilities (four transient states, followed by one absorbing state), this becomes a nonstationary problem. One way to approach this problem is as follows. Since state 5 is an absorbing state, the household's problem in this state is a stationary dynamic programming problem. Bellman's equation for the representative household in state 5, with primes denoting next period values, is:

$$V_5(S) = \max \{(\log c - \gamma n) + \beta E V_5(S')\}$$

subject to the following constraints:

$$TR + (1 - \tau_n)wn + (1 - \tau_k)r_k + (1 + R)b + \delta\tau_k k \geq c + x + b'$$

$$x = k' + (1 - \delta)k$$

$$w = w(K, \lambda, ...), \quad r = r(K, \lambda, ...), \quad X = X(K, \lambda, ...), \quad R = R(K, \lambda, ...)$$

and subject to the laws of motion for government spending and technology.

The state vector s is denoted S and the second constraint in this problem simply restricts prices and aggregate investment to be functions of only aggregate state variables. Since the state 5 problem for the household is stationary, there are a number of ways to solve for state 5 decision rules numerically. Given the special nature of the transition probabilities, the numerical solution to the household's stationary problem for state 5 can be used to solve the household's problem in state 4 (Korean War). In particular, note that Bellman's equation for the household in state 4 is

$$V_4(S) = \max \{ \log(c) - \gamma n + \beta E [\pi(S) V_4(S') +$$

$$(1 - \pi)(S)) V_5(S')] \},$$

where $1 - \pi(S)$ is the state contingent probability of transiting from the Korean War to postwar peace (state 5) in the following period, and $\pi(S)$ is just the probability of remaining in the Korean War (state 4). Given the solution to the stationary state 5 problem, it is now possible to solve the state 4 problem numerically. The solution obtained for the state 4 problem can then be used to solve the household's problem in state 3 (Interwar period) in an analogous fashion, and so forth.

     The solution procedure that is used in this paper is considerably simpler than this five-state method, and is briefly described below. Details on this technique are presented in Appendix A.

     I use a version of Marcet's (1989) procedure of parameterizing expectations, modified by Marcet and Marshall (1992), which operates directly on the Euler equations. Marcet's idea is to solve the expectational Euler equations of the problem by parameterizing them as functions of current-dated state variables. In this case, the right hand sides of the two expectational Euler equations 2.17.iii and 2.17.iv are approximated as $G_1(S)$ and $G_2(S)$, where S is the state vector. Specifically, I follow Marcet's (1989) suggestion and choose G_i to be a power function in the state variables. This yields:

$$(2.18) \quad 1/(1 + R_t) = A_0 \lambda_t^{A_1} K_t^{A_2} g_t^{A_3} d_{wt}^{A_4} d_{kt}^{A_5} \{ \prod_{i=2}^{5} (\psi_{it}^{A_{i+4}}) \}$$

$$(2.19) \quad \phi_t = B_0 \lambda_t^{B_1} K_t^{B_2} g_t^{B_3} d_{wt}^{B_4} d_{kt}^{B_5} \{ \prod_{i=2}^{5} (\psi_{it}^{B_{i+4}}) \}$$

Since $\phi_t = 1/c_t$, note that the decision rules for c_t (and k_{t+1}) can be calculated from the approximating function given by (2.19). The state variables chosen are: (1) the current technology shock (λ); (2) aggregate capital (K); (3) government spending (g); (4) the duration of World War II (d_w), given that the state is ψ_2, where $d_w \in I$, $I \equiv$ set of non-negative integers; (5) the duration of the Korean War ($d_k \in I$), given that the state is ψ_4; and (6) individual indicators of the war/peace state for states $\psi_2,...,\psi_5$. These indicators are required state variables because tax rates and mean government spending are indexed by these states. Given the parameters A_0 and B_0, a separate indicator variable for ψ_1 would be redundant, and in fact, would result in perfect collinearity in the nonlinear regressions used in this procedure that is described below.

It is important to note that this stationary strategy pursued here differs from the procedure described above in that I do not solve first for state 5 decision rules, and then use the state 5 solution to solve for decision rules in the preceding states. I have compared the results from this stationary procedure to the procedure in which decision rules are solved sequentially, and have found very little difference. Based on these results and the fact that the stationary technique is faster than the sequential procedure, I have chosen to work with the stationary technique. This comparison is discussed further in Appendix A.

Given the functional forms for the approximating functions, the initial estimates for the parameters of these functions, draws for the exogenous processes (sequences of technology shocks and government spending shocks), and initial conditions, I impose the aggregate consistency conditions, and iterate on the two Euler equations until the parameters of the two approximating functions converge.

This process results in an approximate competitive equilibrium for this economy, since it yields a system in which the first order conditions for households and firms are satisfied up to approximation error, government debt is priced competitively, and budget constraints, resource constraints and aggregate consistency conditions are satisfied by construction.

An advantage of this method is that the error in the Euler equations can in principle be made arbitrarily small, and it is faster than discretized approaches such as value function iteration.

2.4 MODEL CALIBRATION AND WELFARE COST CALCULATION

Prior to conducting the experiments of interest, values must be assigned to the parameters describing preferences, technology, and government policy variables. For several of these parameters, I choose estimates that have been commonly used in the business cycle and growth literature. I first discuss the parameters governing preferences and technology, followed by government policy parameters. These parameters are listed separately in Appendix B.

The quarterly discount factor, β, is set equal to .99, which delivers a steady state annualized real interest rate of about four percent. The preference parameter γ is fixed at 2.11, which implies that households spend about one-third of their time working in this economy. Similar restrictions have been used by Hansen (1985), and others.

The parameter θ is capital's share of total output, and is fixed at 0.36. This is the value used by Kydland and Prescott (1982), and is almost the middle of the range of estimates for this parameter reported by Christiano (1988). The depreciation rate, δ, is chosen so that the steady state capital-output ratio for the artificial economy matches the average value for the postwar U.S. economy. This implies a value of .0175 or an annual depreciation rate of 7.0 percent. The degree of persistence in the technology shocks, ρ_λ, is set at 0.95, which is the value used by Hansen (1985), Prescott (1986), and Cooley and Hansen (1989). The innovation variance is set to .0076, which is the value used by Prescott. (1986).

The choice of war/peace states and the parameters which describe the transition probabilities across these states are chosen to strike a balance between tractability and a reasonable characterization of the U.S. experience of World War II and the Korean War. For simplicity, P_1 is assumed to be constant; households living in state ψ_1 (peace, pre-World War II) know that in any period, World War II (ψ_2) begins with probability $1 - P_1$. It seems reasonable to model an event such as the outbreak of World War II as a low probability event. Since the solution technique makes use of fixed length simulations, however, problems may arise if P_1 is set extremely close to one. This led me to choose $P_1 = .985$. For this value, the behavior of the prewar economy is qualitatively similar to that of the same economy that is not subject to war, and for each independent simulation, World War II was realized within the first 120 periods.

The sequence $\{P_2\}$ is chosen as follows. First, the mean duration of World War II in the simulated economy is restricted to equal the observed length of World War II, approximately four years. Second, I assume that once World War II begins, the conditional likelihood that the war ends quickly is very low. Given this restriction, and the mean duration restriction, this implies that the likelihood of a very protracted war is very low. This results in the specified sequence $\{P_2\}$ as a function of the duration of the war, with very high initial probabilities that the war continues, and these probabilities decline such that the majority of these simulated wars have durations between 3 and 5 years. The conditional probabilities are generated as $P_2 = \pi_1^{(d-1)(\alpha_1)}$, where $d \equiv$ the duration of the war, and with $\pi_1 = .9999$, and $\alpha_1 = 3.45$. Thus, the longer the war has lasted, the greater the likelihood that the war ends in the following period.

The probability that the Korean War begins $(1 - P_3)$ is also assumed to be constant, and is chosen such that the median duration of peace between the two wars equals the observed interwar duration, which is about four years (1946-1950). For constant P_3, median duration is given by solving for P_3 in the expression $(1 - P_3) * [\sum (P_3)^{16}] = .5$, which yields $P_3 \approx .96$ In this expression, the summation runs over the desired median duration, which is the 16 quarters between 1946-1950. The P_4 sequence is chosen using a strategy similar to that used in constructing $\{P_2\}$. In particular, the unconditional mean duration of the simulated wars is restricted to equal the length of the actual Korean episode (about two years), and conditional probabilities within that state are computed the same way as in World War II. $P_4 = \pi_2^{(d-1)(\alpha_2)}$, with $\pi_2 = .995$, and $\alpha_2 = 3.4$.

The mapping from the five possible states to Government spending and policy choices are as follows. The parameter $v_{gt}(\Psi)$ measures the average level of government purchases indexed by the state. First, postwar federal government spending on goods and services has averaged about 12 percent of GNP. Given steady state output, this pins down average government expenditures (v_g) in states 1 and 5. During the two wars, v_g is set equal to the mean level of government purchases during the specific war episode. This is empirically identified by calculating the average of government expenditure deviations over the war years from a linear-quadratic trend.[7] The trend is estimated using Kendrick's (1961) government spending data from 1890-1957. This fixes v_g for states 2 and 4. v_g For state 3 (the interwar period between World War II and the Korean War) is simply the mean level of government spending during this period, and is also identified as the sample average of deviations from trend.

The parameters ρ_g and σ_{egt}^2 are selected as follows: I fit a first order autoregressive [AR(1)] model to quarterly detrended government expenditures over the postwar period (1953-1990), and calculate the autoregressive parameter, ρ_g. The least squares estimate is 0.93. This is similar to the estimate calculated by Finn (1991) over a similar sample, and is used for all states. This regression also yields an estimate of government expenditure innovation variance $\sigma_{eg}^2 = .0274$, which is used for states 1 and 5. For state 2 in the model (World War II), the sample innovation variance from 1 942-1945 is used. For state 4 in the model, the sample innovation variance from 1950-1953 is used. For state 4, I use the peacetime sample innovation variance.

Joines (1981) has constructed a set of average marginal rates for both capital and labor income taxes. A number of studies have calculated estimates for marginal tax rates, including Barro and Sahasakul (1983), Seater (1985), and Joines (1981). The mapping from states to tax rates is as follows: I set capital and labor income tax rates in the model during Ψ_1, which is the first peacetime state, equal to the average values calculated by Joines for the postwar period. The average marginal peacetime capital tax rate is 50 percent, and the average marginal peacetime labor tax rate is 23 percent. The difference between peacetime steady state tax revenue and peacetime steady state government spending, given the marginal rates of Joines (1981), equals peacetime transfers. During states 2, 3, and 4, (World War II through the Korean War), transfers are set to zero. This seems to be a reasonable approximation, since transfers were negligible during the 1942-1953 period. For World War II and the Korean War (states 2 and 4), labor tax rates and capital tax rates will be set depending on the particular policy considered, and these are described in the following section. For the interwar period, tax rates equal the average values over the 1946-1949 period. For the post-Korean War period, the average values of .23 labor tax and .50 capital tax are adjusted proportionally such that present value budget balance is obtained at the end of 2,000 periods. Increased taxes are required for the postwar period, given that government debt will be issued during war episodes for some of the experiments that are considered.

2.4.1 Welfare Cost Calculation

The approach I use to calculate welfare costs is a widely used one. The basic idea is as follows. Consider two policies, *i* and *j*. If lifetime utility between these two policies differs, then we simply determine how much additional consumption would be required under policy *i* to make the household as well off as under policy *j*. This additional consumption is then a measure of the welfare cost of policy *i*. To implement this approach, I find the value of *x*, which is the required percentage change in consumption , that satisfies the following equation:

$$(2.20) \qquad \sum_{t=0}^{T} \beta^t \left[\log[c_t^*(1+x)] - \gamma n_t^* - \bar{U}_t \right] = 0,$$

where $\bar{U}_t$ is defined as the utility level under the baseline policy: $\log(\bar{c})_t - \gamma \bar{n}_t$. Similar compensation mechanisms have been used by Greenwood and Huffman (1991), and Lucas (1987).

2.5 ECONOMIC ANALYSIS OF GOVERNMENT POLICIES

This section presents quantitative estimates of the economic effects of the different fiscal policies that were used to finance World War II and the Korean War. First, I construct a baseline model that incorporates fiscal policies resembling the actual policies in place during the 1942-1953 period. The welfare cost of the baseline policy is obtained by comparing the present value utility level achieved under this baseline model to that of an economy which did not experience either World War II or the Korean War. This provides an estimate of the costs associated with the resources taken by the government for the war effort (income effects), as well as the costs of the distorting policies used to finance these expenditures (substitution effects). Following the Korean War, the baseline economy, as well as the other economies considered in this section, converges to a stochastic steady state, driven by shocks drawn from the stationary peacetime distributions for government spending and technology.

I then consider the following counterfactual experiments: What would be the consequence if World War II had been financed like the Korean War, or like Britain's World War II under the Keynes plan, in which emphasis was placed on high contemporaneous taxation? Similarly, what if the Korean War had been financed with policies resembling those used to finance World War II?

2.5.1 Construction of the Baseline Model

The first step in establishing the baseline economy is to endow the model with government policies and expenditures that approximate the actual policies and expenditures of the period. To approximate observed policy, I set the labor and capital income tax rates for this period equal to the average values calculated by Joines (1981) for the U.S. between 1941 and 1953. Specifically, the tax rates I use for the baseline model are based on Joines' series "MTRL1," p. 203, and "MTRK1," p. 204. This period includes U.S. participation in World War II, through the end of the Korean War. The marginal labor tax rate averages .20 during World War II, and .2 during the Korean War. The marginal capital tax rate averages .60 during World War II, and .63 during the Korean War. Based on these calculations, it is interesting to note that the Korean War represents the highest level of capital taxation in the history of the U.S. Following the Korean War, the average postwar tax rates of 23% on labor income and 50%

on capital income are adjusted such that present value budget is attained at the end of 2000 periods.

I set the technology shocks during this period such that the pattern roughly approximates the behavior of Kendrick's (1961) total factor productivity series between 1942 and 1953. Kendrick's data indicates a significant rise, on average, in productivity over the first half of the war. The technology shocks selected for these simulations are presented in Figure 1, and are much less variable than those reported by Kendrick. Given the potential measurement error during this period, it seems reasonable to assume a less dramatic increase in total factor productivity than measured in the Kendrick series.[8]

Government spending shocks are also chosen to approximate actual spending during the two wars. As discussed previously in Section 4, I calculate expenditure shocks by subtracting the actual government spending time series between 1941 and 1952 from an estimated least squares quadratic trend. Deviations from trend range between -15 percent (1948), and over 300 percent (1944). Wynne (1990) has used a similar approach in identifying temporary spending shocks, and estimates comparable government expenditure shocks in his study of World War II. Government expenditures for the 1942-1953 period are presented in Figure 2.

The specific solution technique for this economy is detailed in Appendix A. For the experiment of interest, the first step is to set initial conditions. Using Kendrick's (1961) data, I find the U.S. capital stock to be about four percent below trend in 1941, which is the capital stock that consumers are endowed with at the start of World War II. For simplicity, I assume that the public sector has no outstanding claims at the start of the war. The specified government spending and

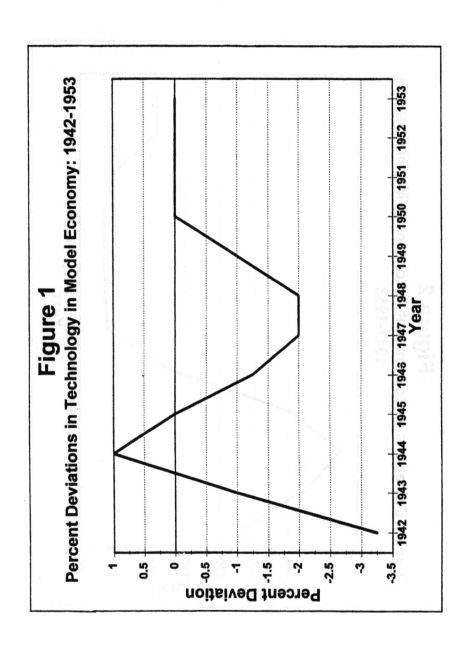

Figure 1
Percent Deviations in Technology in Model Economy: 1942-1953

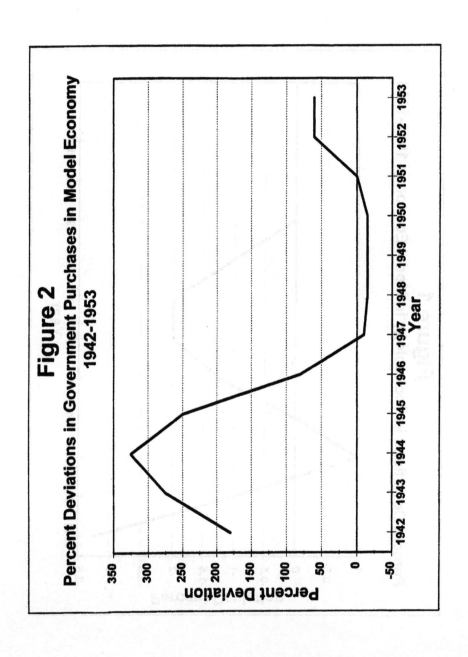

Figure 2
Percent Deviations in Government Purchases in Model Economy
1942-1953

technology shocks are fed into the economy for the 1942-1945 period. Government spending that is not satisfied by capital or labor tax revenue is financed by issuing competitively priced one-period nominal debt, with interest rates being determined by Equation 2.17.iv. Following the Korean War is the absorbing state ψ_s of postwar peace. I let the economy run for 2,000 periods after the end of the Korean War. In the event that the present value of government spending is not equal to the present value of tax revenue at the end of 2,000 periods, postwar labor and capital tax rates are adjusted proportionally until present value budget balance is obtained. The welfare analysis is based on allocations beginning with the start of the war in 1942, and continues over the 2,000 periods following the end of the Korean War. The welfare estimates are based on averages over 100 simulations, in which sequences of i.i.d. government spending and technology shocks are drawn following the Korean War.

2.5.2 Economic Effects of Different War Finance Policies

Figures 3 through 6 display the behavior of output, consumption, the capital stock, and labor supply in the baseline artificial economy during the 1941-1952 period relative to the actual U.S. time series. The actual time series are from Kendrick (1961), and are measured as percent deviations from a quadratic least squares trend; Hodrick-Prescott detrending yields similar results. The distinctive features of the actual time series are the sharp increases in output and labor supply that occurred during World War II, and the more modest increases in these variables during the Korean War. Both consumption and the capital stock fell during World War II, and rose significantly

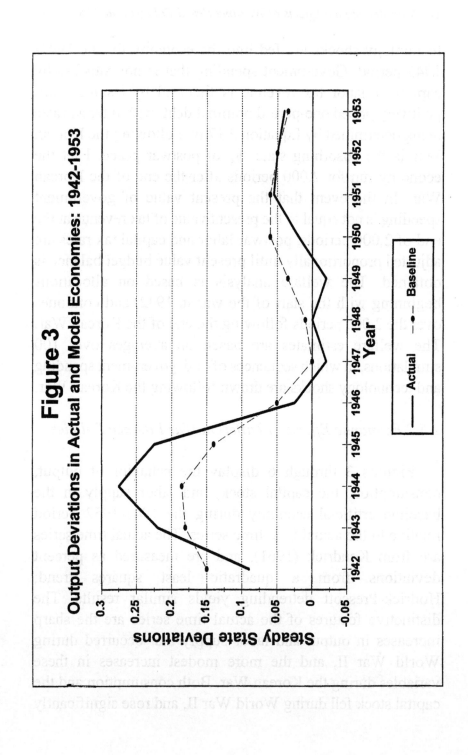

Figure 3

Output Deviations in Actual and Model Economies: 1942-1953

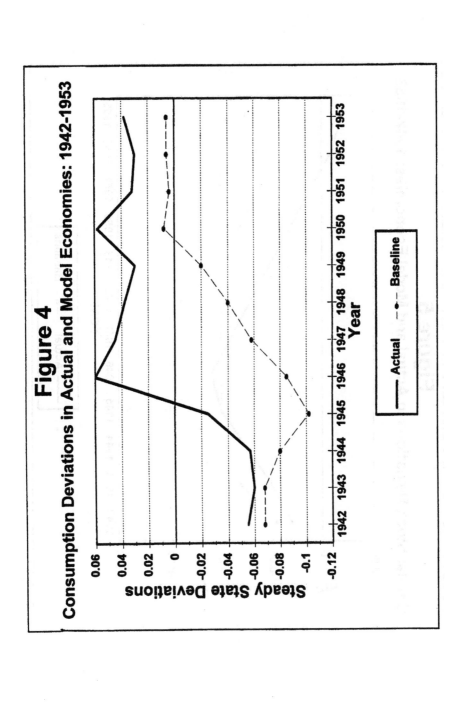

Figure 4

Consumption Deviations in Actual and Model Economies: 1942-1953

Figure 5
Capital Stock Deviations in Actual and Model Economies: 1942-1953

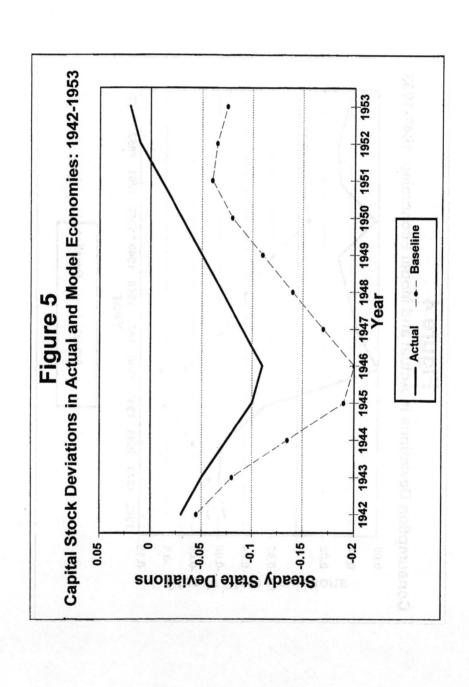

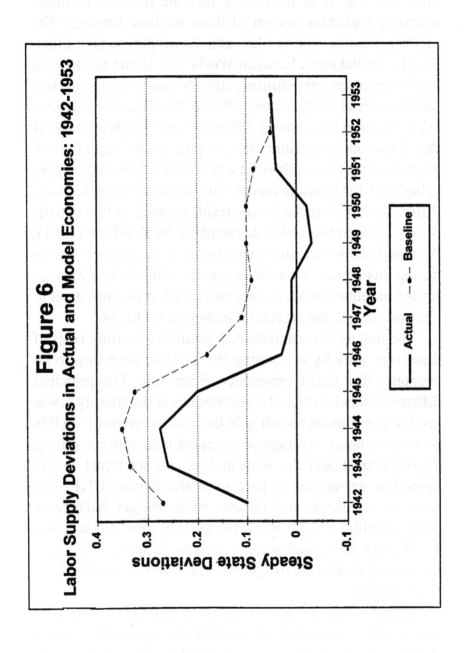

Figure 6
Labor Supply Deviations in Actual and Model Economies: 1942-1953

after the war. It is interesting that the baseline artificial economy replicates several of these wartime features. The model generates very similar paths for output, consumption, and the capital stock between World War II and the Korean model generates very similar paths for output, consumption, and the capital stock between World War II and the Korean War. The most pronounced difference between these series is that deviations in consumption, output, and the capital stock are consistently lower than the actual data, while labor supply is higher in the baseline model. This result likely reflects the difference between the Solow residuals used in this experiment and the Solow residuals calculated by Kendrick (1961). As noted above, measurement error may be relatively large during this period. To achieve present value budget balance for the baseline model, the tax rate on labor income is set to .26, and the tax rate on capital income is set to .54.

The first welfare exercise is to estimate the utility costs of these two wars by comparing the baseline economy to an economy that didn't experience either war. The principal difference between these two economies is the sharply lower level of government spending in the no-war economy. In this no-war economy, average government expenditures during World War II and the Korean War are set equal to the peacetime average of 12 percent of steady state GNP. Tax rates are constant, and present value budget balance is achieved with lower tax rates. The labor income tax rate is set to .21, and the capital income tax rate is set to .47. Since technology shocks are exogenous, they are identical in these two exercises.

I find that a permanent, six percent increase in consumption, which is equivalent to more than four percent of steady state GNP, is required to compensate individuals in this economy with World War II and the Korean War financed under the baseline policy. This compensation is comparable to the benefits associated with several hypothetical major tax reforms evaluated by Cooley and Hansen (1990) in a deterministic version of a similar economy. For example, Cooley and Hansen calculate the benefit from permanently replacing all capital tax revenue with higher labor income taxes to be about six percent of GNP. Similarly, the benefit from permanently replacing all labor income taxes with lump sum taxes is about five percent of GNP.

It is also possible to calculate the welfare costs of these two wars individually. The welfare cost of World War II under the baseline policy is compensated by a permanent increase of nearly five percent in consumption, while the welfare cost of the Korean War is compensated by a permanent increase of about one percent in consumption.

Experiment two, which is summarized in Table 3, evaluates the implications of financing World War II with balanced budget-type fiscal policies similar to those used during the Korean War. It is important to note that it is not possible to finance World War II in this model exclusively with revenue from distorting taxes; maximum tax revenue is considerably less than World War government expenditures.

For this high-tax experiment, I choose the tax policy that maximizes the present value of World War II tax revenues. To identify this policy, I simply search over various combinations of labor and capital income tax rates during World War II. Since tax rates in the baseline model are constant and indexed by the state, $\tau_{jt} = \tau_{ji}(\psi_1); j = \{k,n\}, \psi_1 \in \Psi$, the search is conducted over tax rate combination that are also constant during the war.[9] I find that maximum present value capital and labor tax revenue is obtained by setting labor income taxes during World War II to 34 percent, and capital

Table 3

Welfare Costs of Alternative Policies

Averages over 100 Simulations

Policy	τ_n	τ_k	Welfare Cost of War Policies
No Wars	.210	.470	0.0%
Baseline Policy			6.0%
WWII	.190	.600	
Korea	.200	.630	
Postwar	.260	.540	
Korean Policy			11.0%
WWII	.340	.890	
Korea	.200	.630	
Postwar	.240	.510	
WWII Policy			5.6%
WWII	.190	.600	
Korea	.240	.510	
Postwar	.266	.546	

income taxes to 89 percent. Competitively priced one-period debt is issued to satisfy remaining government expenditures. Note that the baseline Korean tax policy is not changed for this experiment.

I find that these temporary wartime increases in labor and capital income taxes have large positive and normative effects. Figures 7 through 10 present the paths of steady state deviations in output, consumption, capital stock, and labor supply for the baseline economy and the Korean war-financed economy financed with high taxes during both World War II and the Korean War. Consumption falls quickly, which reflects a relatively high beginning-of-war capital stock and very high capital tax rates. Perhaps the most significant difference between the two economies is the behavior of the capital stock. Physical capital in the baseline model is approximately 18 percent below the steady state at the end of the war in 1946, while it declines nearly 60 percent under the high tax policy. Labor input, which rises sharply in the baseline case, averages about 25 percent below the steady state in the high tax economy. There are very large differences in output between the two economies. Peak output in the high-tax economy is about 10 percent below the steady state, but is over 20 percent above the steady state in the baseline economy. Consumption falls to about 12 percent below the steady state in the baseline economy, but declines over 35 percent in the high-tax economy.

While the marginal cost of this high tax policy is the severe distortions imposed on households during World War II, the marginal benefit is that war debt in this high tax economy is significantly lower than in the baseline policy. This allows lower postwar tax rates of about 24% on labor income, and 51% on capital income. The benefit of lower

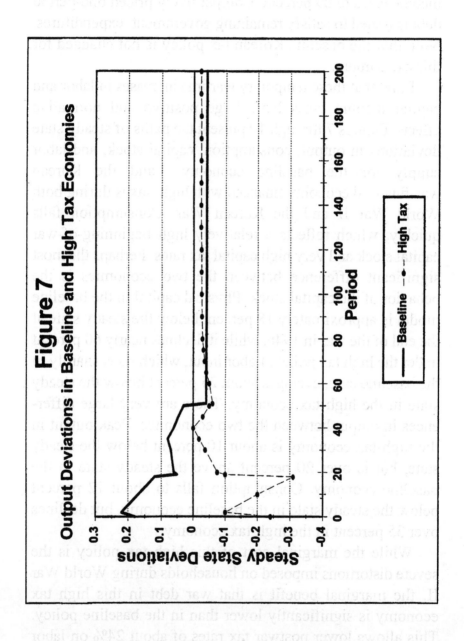

Figure 7

Output Deviations in Baseline and High Tax Economies

Baseline —•— High Tax

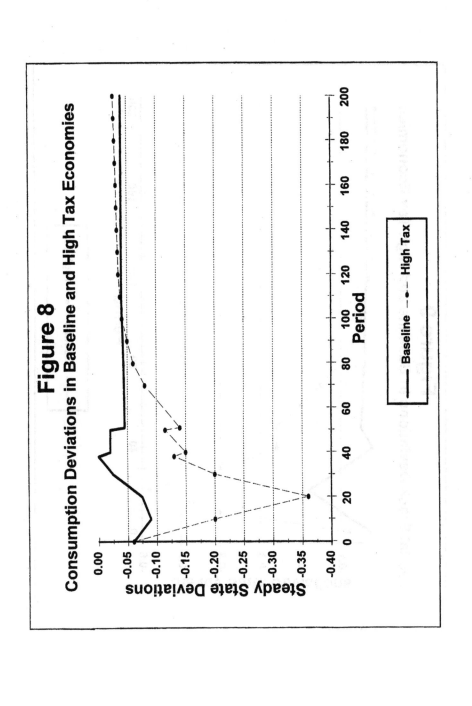

Figure 8
Consumption Deviations in Baseline and High Tax Economies

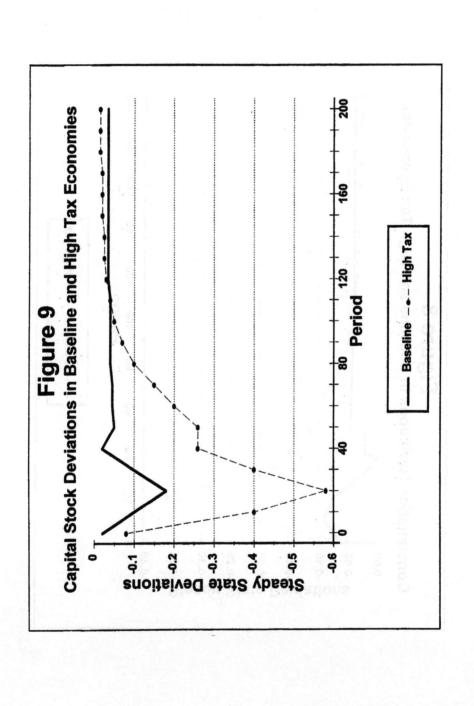

Figure 9

Capital Stock Deviations in Baseline and High Tax Economies

Baseline —— High Tax —•—

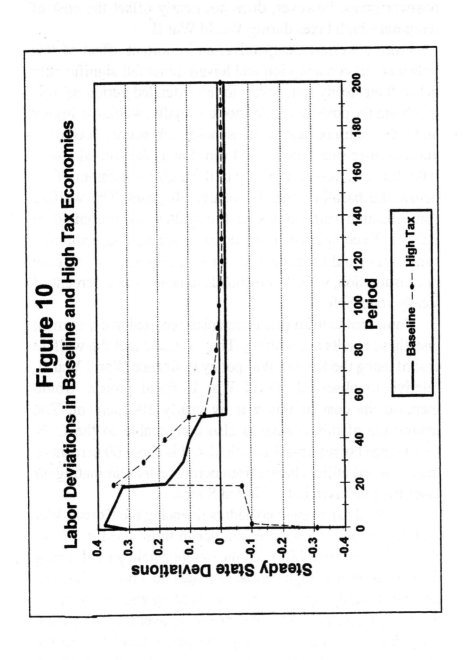

Figure 10

Labor Deviations in Baseline and High Tax Economies

postwar taxes, however, does not nearly offset the cost of temporary high taxes during World War II.

From a welfare perspective, an important effect of this policy is that consumption and leisure must fall significantly below their steady state levels for an extended period of time to rebuild the postwar capital stock. Initially, welfare is higher under the high-tax case, as households substitute out of market activities into leisure, and run down the capital stock. After the war, however, utility in the high-tax economy falls below the baseline case for nearly 30 years. The welfare compensation calculations of this policy are presented in Table 3. To compensate individuals in this high tax economy, consumers would require a permanent, four percent increase in consumption, which corresponds to nearly three percent of steady state GNP.

Compared to the utility differences reported in experiment one, these results are striking. They indicate that the welfare cost of using the Korean War policy to finance World War II, relative to observed World War II fiscal policy, would increase the cost of this war by nearly 100 percent. The magnitude of this change is also comparable to the Cooley-Hansen tax reforms. In particular, it is about 60 percent of the estimated utility change from permanently eliminating *all* labor income taxes in the United States.

The third experiment considers financing the Korean War with tax-smoothing policies similar to those used in World War II. I consider a shift from the baseline policy used during the Korean War of high capital tax rates, to a policy that sets tax rates roughly equal to postwar counterparts. To construct the new policy, labor tax rates are set to average 24 percent, and capital tax rates to average 51 percent, relative to the baseline Korean War tax rates of 20 percent, and 63 percent, respectively. Competitively priced nominal debt during the

Korean War is higher under this policy relative to the baseline model, and as a result, higher postwar taxes are required for present value budget balance. Postwar labor taxes are set to about 27%, and postwar capital taxes are set to about 55%.

Figure 11 displays steady state deviations in output in the baseline and tax-smoothing economies during the Korean War. At the start of the Korean War, output under the tax smoothing policy is about four percentage points above output in the baseline economy, and remains above baseline output over the course of the war. Figure 14 presents labor supply deviations under these two policies, and the differences here are nearly identical to those in output. Consumption and the capital stock, which are presented in Figures 12 and 13, are also higher under the alternative policy. It is interesting to note that the capital stock remains above baseline capital for 15 years following the end of the war. Given that higher postwar taxes are required under the alternative policy, steady state consumption, labor supply, and capital are lower than the steady state counterparts under the baseline model. Higher labor supply under the tax-smoothing policy results in lower utility during the Korean War. This reflects a higher capital stock following the end of the war, which results in higher consumption and leisure during the transition to the new steady state.

Table 3 presents the welfare difference between these two economies. I estimate that a permanent 0.4 percent increase in consumption, which corresponds to about 25 billion current dollars, is required to raise present value utility under the baseline policy to the level attained under the alternative tax-smoothing policy. This suggests that the relative cost of the Korean War could have been reduced by about 40 percent, from one percent of GNP to about 0.6 percent of GNP, by adopting the alternate policy. While this utility difference is

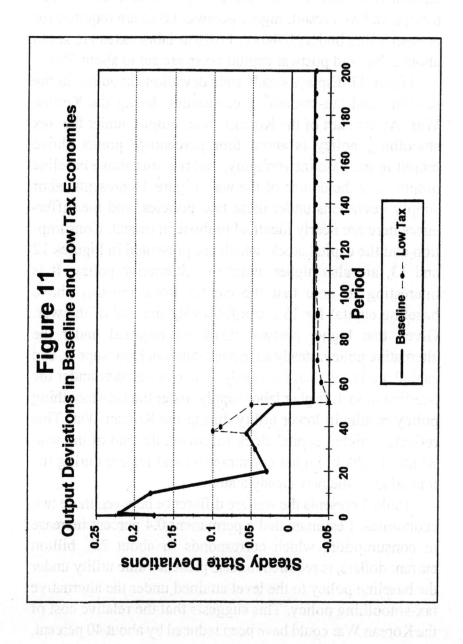

Figure 11

Output Deviations in Baseline and Low Tax Economies

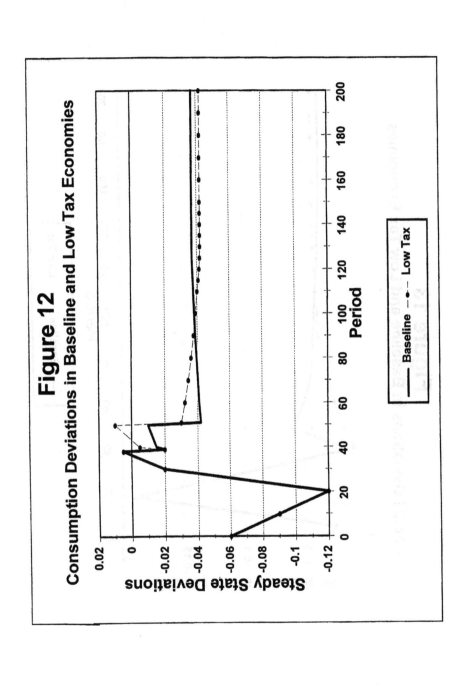

Figure 12
Consumption Deviations in Baseline and Low Tax Economies

Baseline —•— Low Tax

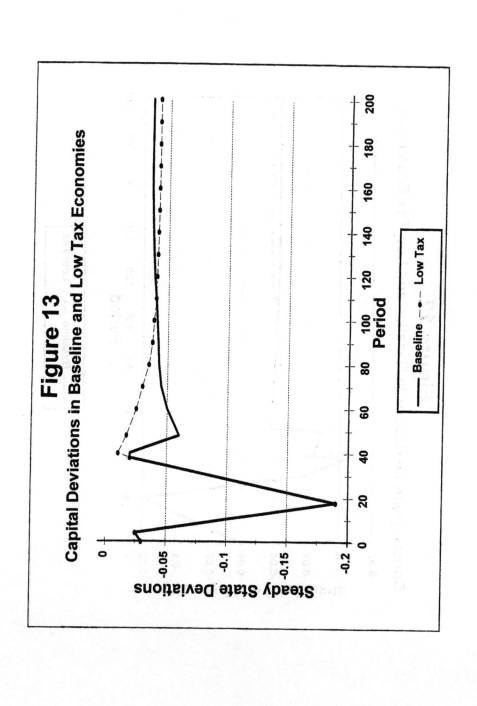

Figure 13

Capital Deviations in Baseline and Low Tax Economies

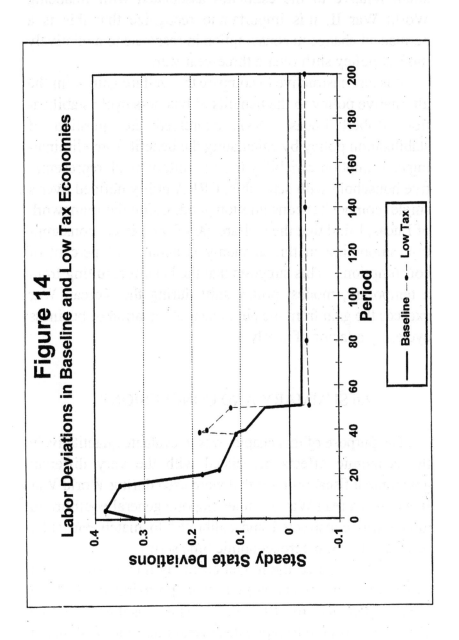

Figure 14

Labor Deviations in Baseline and Low Tax Economies

small relative to the estimates associated with financing World War II, it is important to recognize that this is a permanent change in consumption in response to a relatively modest policy shift over a three-year war.

It is also instructive to compare the welfare gain from the alternative policy to the benefits of business cycle stabilization. Robert Lucas (1987) addressed the question of stabilization policy by calculating the benefit from eliminating consumption variability to an infinitely lived, representative household with separable, CRRA utility defined over a single (composite) consumption good. Using the framework of Lucas, I find that the welfare gain from perfect consumption smoothing in this economy is about 0.14 percent of consumption.[10] This suggests that the benefit resulting from a temporary, modest policy shift during the Korean War exceeds the gain from the permanent elimination of business cycles by a factor of nearly 3.

2.6 SUMMARY AND CONCLUSIONS

The purpose of this chapter was to evaluate quantitatively the economic effects associated with the very different government fiscal policies that were used during World War II and the Korean War. An intertemporal general equilibrium model was constructed and calibrated to match particular features of U.S. macroeconomic time series.

I first simulated the model economy under government expenditure shocks and policies that approximate the actual U.S. experience of 1941-1953. This baseline artificial economy was able to replicate several important features of the data, including the substantial increases in labor supply and output that occurred during World War II. Several counterfactual experiments were conducted to assess the welfare costs and other economic effects of different wartime fiscal policies. The first compared the baseline economy to an economy that was not engaged in either World War II or the Korean War. I found that the welfare cost of these two years, including the policies used to finance them, was about five percent of consumption, with most of this loss due to World War II.

The second experiment analyzed the effects of financing World War II with balanced-budget policies similar to those used during the Korean War. I found that a permanent, four percent increase in consumption was required to compensate households under the Korean War policy for World War II. This cost is very high, and reflects the sharp increase in labor and capital income taxation associated with a policy that maximizes contemporaneous tax revenue from labor and capital income. The behavior of macroeconomic variables under this policy is strikingly different. Labor supply and output both fall considerably, and the capital stock declines nearly sixty percent. This sharp drop in capital results in a persistent decline in leisure and consumption as individuals rebuild the capital stock back to the steady state level.

During the Korean War, President Truman hoped to maintain a balanced budget, "even if military costs doubled", and stated "Our (the American) people understand that if we had paid higher taxes in World War II we would be better off today." [Studenski and Kroos (1963), page 493.] However, if the balanced budget policy Truman advocated was Pareto-superior to actual World War II policy, it clearly must be through some channels not evident within the neoclassical growth model used in this paper.

The third experiment examines the behavior of the economy if tax-smoothing policies in the spirit of World War

II were used to finance the Korean War. A policy of lower capital taxes and somewhat higher labor taxes during the Korean episode is estimated to have provided a permanent benefit to households equal to 0.4 percent of consumption. While this calculation is small relative to the World War II experiment, it suggests that the costs of the Korean War could have been reduced about 60 percent by a relatively modest policy change. Moreover, the welfare gain arising from the alternative policy appears to be substantial relative to estimated gains from business cycle stabilization in this economy.

III

The Macroeconomic Effects
of World War II Monetary Policy:
Price Controls, Rationing, and Inflation

3.1 INTRODUCTION

In this chapter, the analysis of the macroeconomic effects of war finance is extended to study issues associated with wartime monetary policies. As discussed in Chapter 1, an important feature of many war episodes in the U.S. and other countries is the use of the inflation tax to help finance war expenditures. Frequently, however, governments have also adopted general price controls during wars in conjunction with high inflation policies. Typically, these controls impose maximum legal nominal prices on goods and services that are often well below market-clearing prices. With prices set below market clearing levels, this policy results in excess demand, and leads governments to adopt some form of rationing. Price controls were adopted by the U.S. during the Revolutionary War, World War I, the Korean war, the Vietnam War, and were used extensively during World War II by the U.S. and several European countries.

Analyzing the effects of money with prices that are not always at market clearing levels has a long tradition in macroeconomics. One strategy in this literature that has been pursued by Barro and Grossman (1976), Benassy (1982), Grandmont (1982), and others is to model economies with fixed prices as explicit disequilibrium situations, in which prices fixed below (above) equilibrium results in excess demand (supply), and output is determined on the short side of the market: $Q_i = \min[Q_i^S(p,...), Q_i^d(p,...)]$, where Q_i is the quantity of good i consumed, Q^S is quantity supplied given the row price vector p, and Q^d is the quantity demanded given the row price vector p. This strategy implies that firms will not sell all that is demanded at a low, controlled price. The analysis that will be developed in this chapter is in the spirit of this disequilibrium literature.

The focus of this chapter is to study the effects of monetary policy in a wartime economy that is subject to temporary general price controls and rationing. An inter-temporal monetary model will be used to analyze the experience of the U.S. economy during World War II, which is a period of extensive price controls, broad-based rationing, and rapid money supply growth.

Many economists [e.g., Evans (1982)] have criticized the use of general price controls and rationing. In particular, it has been noted that the adoption of controls is inefficient as individuals form queues to buy goods, or use resources to avoid controls. Evans has estimated that if prices were allowed to clear markets during World War II, employment would have been 11 percent higher and output seven percent higher by the end of the war. These estimates are inferred from money demand and labor force participation that were estimated over World War II, using regression methods. They are not, however, derived from an explicit optimizing model.

The positive question of "What are the economic effects of price controls?," posed by Evans and others, can be studied in this framework by solving the model economy for a flexible price equilibrium, and comparing it to the solution of the model under price controls and rationing. In particular, the model can be used to evaluate whether the reduced form estimates reported by Evans are consistent with results from an explicit, intertemporal, optimizing environment.

A second important issue associated with the monetary policy used during World War II is the huge postwar inflation of 1946-1948. Between the end of the war and 1948, wholesale prices rose nearly 60 percent. Since government debt is denominated in nominal terms, one important effect of this inflation was a decline in the real value of the stock of public debt. The increase in the price level and resulting fall in the value of government debt was equivalent to a repudiation of debt equal to nearly 40 percent of GNP. Abstracting from time-consistency and reputational issues, there are potentially important welfare issues associated with this "capital levy." As Lucas and Stokey (1983) have pointed out, if explicit lump sum taxes are not available to the government, it can be welfare-enhancing to reduce debt by a surprise inflation relative to a policy of paying off the debt by raising distorting taxes. To estimate the long-run effects of the post-World War II inflation, I construct a counterfactual experiment in which the debt is fully honored by raising distorting taxes on factor incomes, and compute the welfare differences between this policy and the observed experience of the high postwar inflation. Section 3.2 presents some key features associated with historical monetary policy during historical war episodes. Section 3.3 describes briefly the price control and rationing schemes used in World War II. The model economy is developed in Section 3.4, and calibrated in Section 3.6. Results of the equilibrium and controlled economies are presented in Section 3.6. The counterfactual results of the surprise inflation are analyzed in Section 3.7.

3.2 MONETARY POLICIES DURING U.S. WARS AND DESIGN OF COUNTERFACTUAL POLICY

Figures 15 and 16 plot U.S. wholesale prices between 1800 and 1948, and 1800 and 1991 (log scale), respectively. These data reveal an interesting pattern of historical wartime monetary policies in the U.S., which involve significant inflation during the war, followed by a return to the prewar price level. For example, the sharp inflation that occurred during the War of 1812 is seen clearly in Figure 15. Prices rose quickly during the war, with the price level rising about 50 percent between 1812 and 1815. Following the war, the price level returned to its prewar level by 1818. Similar policy occurred during the Civil War. The price level in the Union roughly doubled during the Civil War (1861-1865), but again returned ultimately to its prewar level by 1880. A similar inflationary policy was in place during World War I, as prices doubled between 1917 and 1919. A sharp deflation during 1920-21, however, returned prices nearly to prewar levels.

Evidence from these wars suggests that the typical pattern of monetary policy during a conflict was to inflate the economy significantly during the war to help pay for the war effort, then deflate the economy back to the old price level following the end of the war.

At first, monetary policy during World War II resembled policy in other war episodes. Money growth (M1) on average rose about 18 percent per year, and despite the imposition of general price controls, measured inflation averaged about seven percent. Following the war, however, government behavior differed strikingly from the deflationary policies used immediately after the War of 1812, the Civil War and

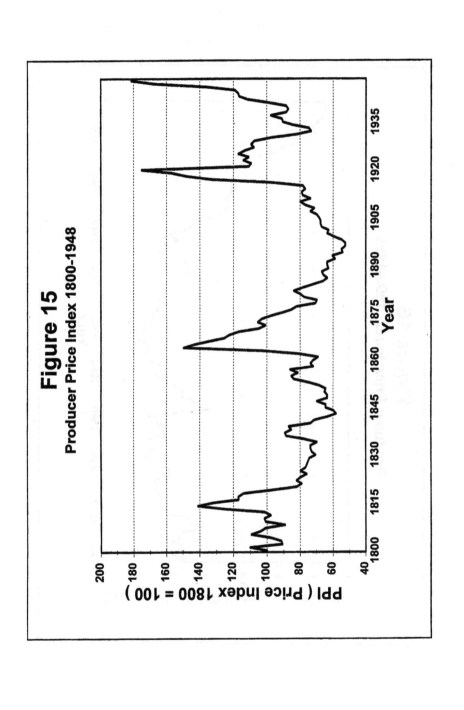

Figure 15
Producer Price Index 1800-1948

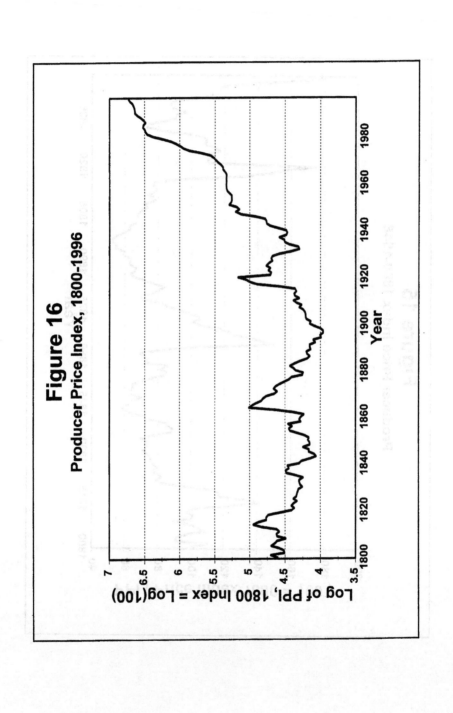

Figure 16

Producer Price Index, 1800-1996

World War I. Rather than deflating the economy back to the prewar price level, prices rose substantially after World War II, with the price level rising about 60 percent between 1946 and 1948.

Since government debt is denominated in dollars, one important effect of the post-World War II inflation is a large reduction in the real value of the outstanding national debt. By partially repudiating the public debt, this inflation acted much like a "capital levy". To study the long-run effect of this surprise inflation, I will conduct a counterfactual experiment in which a deflationary monetary policy is chosen following World War II.

The design of the postwar deflationary policy used in the counterfactual experiment is guided by the behavior of wholesale prices following these earlier U.S. wars. The deflationary policy is constructed such that immediately following the war, the price level declines gradually from its peak back to its prewar value. Given the sharp decline in output that occurs immediately following the war, this requires a substantial reduction in the money stock in the first postwar period. This withdrawal is accomplished by the government selling debt to households in exchange for currency. Starting in the second postwar period, money is withdrawn from the economy at a constant rate for N periods such that in the new steady state, the price level is equal to the old prewar level. The specific nature of this deflationary policy is described in Section 2.5.

This experiment is used to study the implications of following the typical historical postwar policy after World War II. Since nominal government debt is not debased in this experiment, public debt is fully honored by raising revenue from distorting taxes on factor incomes. The outcome of this deflationary experiment can be compared to the results from the economy under government policies that approximate the actual high inflation policies that were in place after the war.

3.3 WORLD WAR II RATIONING
AND PRICE CONTROLS

General price controls and various rationing schemes have been used during several U.S. wars, and have been documented in detail by Rockoff (1984). The office of price administration (OPA) was established in late 1941, and in April, 1942, General Maximum Price Regulation (GMPR) was passed, freezing prices at the highest levels reached in March, 1942. Rockoff reports that GMPR was modified by the OPA over the course of the war by attempting to fine tune controls across various industries. By November 1946, nearly all price controls had been removed. Since regulated prices for many commodities were below market clearing prices, goods were rationed. Ration "coupons," or tickets, were issued to households, allowing the coupon holder to purchase up to a specific quantity of a commodity at a price not to exceed the maximum legal price. Rationed commodities included food, clothing, energy, housing (rents), and transportation [see Rockoff, p. 128 and p. 133].

Not surprisingly, black markets developed during World War II. By 1944, nearly 340,000 violations of controls/rationing had been compiled by the OPA, [Rockoff, p. 143], and black market prices for meat were reported to be double the maximum legal price [Rockoff, p. 149]. Rockoff notes that in the middle Atlantic region, nearly all poultry transactions involved the black market. By its very nature, it is very difficult to estimate the size of the black market during World War II. These data suggest, however, that it was not insignificant.

3.4 THE MODEL ECONOMY

To construct the model economy, the environment used in Chapter 2 is extended to include a role for valued fiat money by restricting purchases of the consumption good (c_t) to be subject to a cash-in-advance (CIA) constraint; all consumption purchases can only be satisfied with pre-accumulated cash.

A more flexible variant of this model is to use Lucas and Stokey's (1983) distinction between cash and credit goods, in which certain goods (credit goods) can be purchased with contemporaneously earned income. This framework has been used by Cooley and Hansen (1990), who estimate that for the post-World War II period, credit goods appear to be a relatively small component of total consumption.

Preferences for the representative household are given by:

$$(3.1) \qquad \sum_{t=0}^{\infty} \beta^t (\log c_t - \gamma n_t) \quad 0 < \beta < 1.$$

c_t is consumption and n_t is the fraction of time spend working, and β is the household's subjective discount factor. Hours worked for the representative household enters utility linearly, as in Hansen (1985).

Following Lucas (1982), each period in this model economy is divided into two subperiods. In the first subperiod, the asset market opens for trade. During this period, households may trade claims with the government and with other households. However, since households are identical, there will be no claims issued across households in equilibrium. Households may purchase government debt, and it is assumed that only nominally risk-free one-period government debt is issued. Consumers enter the asset market with beginning of period money holdings m_t. They collect principal and interest on matured one-period guaranteed government debt that is denominated in dollars, $(1 + R_t)b_t$, and use those proceeds to purchase new government debt, b_{t+1}. At the conclusion of these transactions, the asset market closes. This leaves the household with $m_t + (1 + R_t)b_t - b_{t+1}$ units of currency, which can be used to purchase the consumption good, c_t in the following product market, or can be held by the household for use the following period.

Consumers maximize (3.1) subject to the following sequence of wealth constraints:

$$
(3.2) \quad
\begin{aligned}
&TR_t + (1 + R_t)b_t/p_t + (1 - \delta)k_t + (1 - r_{kt})r_t k_t + \tau_{kt}\delta k_t + \\
&m_t/p_t + (1 - \tau_{nt})w_t n_t \geq k_{t+1} + b_{t+1}/p_t + c_t + m_{t+1}/p_t
\end{aligned}
$$

and also subject to the sequence of cash-in-advance constraints:

$$
(3.3) \quad m_t/p_t + (1 + R_t)b_t/p_t - b_{t+1}/p_t \geq c_t
$$

(3.3) will bind, provided that nominal interest rates are strictly positive. Each period, households purchase consumption (c_t) and new government debt (b_{t+1}), and carry forward next period's capital stock (k_{t+1}) and money stock (m_{t+1}). Funding for these purchases includes after-tax labor income $[(1 - \tau_{nt})w_t n_t]$, where w_t is the period t wage rate and n_t is hours worked, and after-tax capital income net of depreciation $[(1 - \tau_{kt})r_t k_t + \delta\tau_{kt}k_t]$, where r_t is the real rental rate of capital and the term $\delta\tau_{kt}k_t$ captures the depreciation effect in the tax code. Remaining wealth is given by beginning-of-period money holdings (m_t/p_t), transfers from the government (TR_t), and principal and interest on matured government debt $[(1 + R_t)b_t/p_t]$.

Household investment is defined as:

$$(3.4) \qquad x_t = k_{t+1} - (1 - \delta)k_t$$

A competitive firm produces output from the Cobb-Douglas production function:

$$(3.5) \qquad Y_t = \lambda_t K_t^\theta N_t^{1-\theta}, \quad 0 < \theta < 1.$$

Capital letters indicate per capital quantities, which competitive households view parametrically. In equilibrium, household choices will equal per capital quantities. λ_t, which is the current level of technology, is given exogenously by the sequence $\{\lambda_t\}_{t=0}^\infty$. It is assumed households know λ_t with perfect foresight.

Given constant returns to scale, profit maximization by the firm will yield zero profits, and implies the following functions for wage and rental rates:

(3.6) $w(K_t, N_t, \lambda_t) = \lambda_t (1 - \theta)[K_t / N_t]^\theta$

(3.7) $r(K_t, N_t, \lambda_t) = \lambda_t \theta [N_t / K_t]^{1-\theta}.$

Government exists to finance a non-negative sequence of required exogenous expenditures $\{g_t\}_{t=0}^\infty$. Following Lucas and Stokey (1983), I assume that government expenditures do not enter utility functions or enhance private sector productivity. Government spending is satisfied by capital and labor tax revenue, and by issuing nominal debt.   To focus on the effects of monetary policy during World War II, the peace/war states developed in Chapter 1 are simplified considerably. In this application, I abstract from the Korean War and from pre-World War II considerations that were studied earlier. Two states are now chosen to approximate an economy that is subjected to World War II, followed by peace:

ψ_1: World War II

ψ_2: Postwar Peace

I assume that the war is known to last T periods, and that state ψ_2 is an absorbing state.

Government spending and tax rates are functions of the peace/war state. $G_t(\Psi) = \{G_{1t}(\psi_1), G_2(\psi_2)\}$, where G_{1t} is required government spending during World War II, and G_2 is required government spending in peace. Labor and capital tax rates are given analogously:

$$\tau_{nt}(\Psi) = \left\{\tau_{n1}(\psi_1), \tau_{n2}(\psi_2)\right\}, \quad \tau_{kt}(\Psi) = \left\{\tau_{k1}(\psi_1), \tau_{k2}(\psi_2)\right\}.$$

The values assigned to the sequences $\{g_t\}$, τ_{kt}, and $\{\tau_{nt}\}$ are discussed in Section 5. Monetary policy in this economy consists simply of setting $\{M_t\}_{t=0}^{\infty}$. During the war, the money stock will be set to the average money growth observed during World War II.

For the counterfactual experiment in which World War II debt is fully honored, monetary policy will be conducted by withdrawing money from the economy to approximate the average historical postwar policy of deflating the economy back to the prewar price level from the peak price level reached during the last period of the war. For the alternative experiment in which unexpected high postwar inflation partially repudiates the war debt, households will behave as if they know with certainty that the government will follow a deflationary postwar monetary policy.

I define a feasible government policy as one in which the present value of government expenditures and transfers equals the present value of government revenue:

$$\sum_{t=0}^{\infty} \left\{ \left(\prod_{t=0}^{\infty} [1/(1+R_t)] \right) [G_t + TR_t \right.$$

$$\left. - \tau_{nt} w_t N_t - \ell_t - \tau_{kt}(r_t - \delta) K_t] \right\} = 0,$$

(3.10)

where ℓ_t is defined as seignorage: $\ell_t \equiv (m_{t+1} - m_t)/p_t$.

The period government budget constraint is given by:

$$G_t + TR_t + (1 + R_t)B_t / p_t =$$

(3.11)

$$\tau_{nt} w_t N_t + \tau_{kt}(r_t - \delta)K_t + B_{t+1}/p_t + \ell_t$$

The resource constraint for this economy is given by:

(3.12) $$\lambda_t K_t^\theta N_t^{1-\theta} \geq C_t + X_t + G_t$$

Given initial endowments of capital, bonds, a feasible government policy, and a law of motion for government debt, a perfect foresight competitive equilibrium for this economy consists of sequences for nominal goods prices $\{p_t\}_{t=0}^\infty$, nominal interest rates $\{R_t\}_{t=0}^\infty$, factor prices, $\{w_t, r_t\}_{t=0}^\infty$ and household allocations $\{m_{t+1}, k_{t+1}, b_{t+1}, n_t, c_t\}_{t=0}^\infty$, such that:

(1) Given the sequence of goods prices, interest rates, and factor prices, the sequence of allocations maximizes (3.1) subject to the constraints (3.2) and (3.3);

(2) Factor prices satisfy the firm efficiency conditions (3.6) and (3.7);

(3) Nominal interest rates satisfy the pricing relation

$$1/(1 + R_{t+1}) =$$

$$[(1 - \tau_{kt+1})r_{t+1} + (1 - \delta) + \delta\tau_{kt+1}]p_{t+1}/p_t;$$

This guarantees that nominal government debt is priced competitively, and implies that households will hold the outstanding stock of government debt in equilibrium.

(4) Allocations are feasible, and household choices of consumption (c_t), bonds (b_{t+1}), money (m_{t+1}), capital (k_{t+1}), and effort (n_t), coincide with aggregate outcomes:

$$c_t = C_t, \; b_{t+1} = B_{t+1}, \; m_{t+1} = M_{t+1}, \; k_{t+1} = K_{t+1}, \text{ and } n_t = N_t.$$

This last requirement is also known as an aggregate consistency condition.

The focus of this exercise will be to analyze the behavior of this economy subjected to World War II, and then solve for the transition path to a new steady state following the end of the war. The steady state in ψ_2 will be characterized by constant government spending, taxes, money, and technology.

Note that for both the counterfactual experiment in which money is withdrawn from the economy following the end of the war to restore the prewar price level, and the surprise high inflation experiment, households behave as if they know with certainty that the government will follow the historical deflationary policy.

3.4.1 Approximating the Competitive Equilibrium

For the absorbing post-World War II state, (ψ_2), Bellman's equation for the representative household is:

$$V_{2t}(S_{2t}) = \max \{ (\log c_t - \gamma n_t) + \beta V_{2t+1}(S_{2t+1}) \}$$

subject to:

$$m_t/p_t + TR_t + (1 - \tau_{nt})w_t n_t + (1 - \tau_{kt})r_t k_t$$

$$+ (1 + R_t)b_t/p_t + \delta\tau_{kt}k_t \geq$$

$$c_t + x_t + b_{t+1}/p_t + m_{t+1}/p_t,$$

$$m_t/p_t + (1 + R_t)b_t/p_t \geq c_t + b_{t+1}/p_t,$$

$$p = p(K, M, ...) \quad w = w(K, M, ...)$$

$$r_t = r_t(K_t, M_t, ...) \quad R_t = R_t(K_t, M_t, ...)$$

$$X_t = X_t(K_t, M_t, ...).$$

The last two constraints restrict aggregate investment (X_t) and prices (P_t, r_t, R_t, w_t), to be functions of only aggregate state variables, and not individual household state variables. The household's state vector S_2 is defined as $\{k_t, K_t, b_t, B_t, m_t, M_t, D_t\}$. The state vector consists of household and aggregate capital, bonds, and money. D_t is a vector summarizing the postwar deflationary policy. Postwar technology, government expenditures, and tax rates are assumed to be constant.

Now, consider the household's problem during the war. Noting that World War II lasts T periods, Bellman's equation for the representative household for $t = 1, ..., T - 1$ is:

$$V_{1t}(S_{1t}) = \max \{ (\log c_t - \gamma n_t) + \beta V_{1t+1}(s_{1t+1}) \}$$

and for period T, is given by

$$V_{1T}(S_{1T}) = \max\{(\log c_T - \gamma n_T) + \beta V_2(S_{2T+1})\}$$

subject to:

$$m_t/p_t + TR_t + (1 - \tau_{nt})w_t n_t + (1 - \tau_{kt})r_t k_t$$

$$+ (1 + R_t)b_t/p_t + \delta\tau_{kt}k_t \geq$$

$$c_t + x_t + b_{t+1}/p_t + m_{t+1}/p_t,$$

$$m_t/p_t + (1 + R_t)b_t/p_t \geq c_t + b_{t+1}/p_t,$$

$$p = p(K, M, ...) \quad w = w(K, M, ...)$$

$$r_t = r_t(K_t, M_t, ...) \quad R_t = R_t(K_t, M_t, ...)$$

$$X_t = X_t(K_t, M_t, ...).$$

The state vector during the war (S_{1t}), $t \leq T$, is defined as $\{k_t, K_t, b_t, B_t, \{\bar{\lambda}_t\}, \{\bar{G}_t\}, m_t, \{M_t\}\}$, where $\{\bar{\lambda}_t\}$ is defined as the $1 \times (T + 1 - t)$ vector of current and future technology levels corresponding to the remaining periods in the war: $[\lambda_t, ... \lambda_T]$, $\{\bar{g}_t\}$ is defined as the $1 \times (T + 1 - t)$ vector of current and future government spending requirements corresponding to the remaining periods in the war: $[G_t, ... G_T]$, and similarly, $\{\bar{M}_t\}$ is defined as the $1 \times (T + 1 - t)$ vector of current and future money supplies corresponding to the remaining periods in the war: $[M_t, ..., M_t]$.

Denoting ϕ_t to be the date–t multiplier associated with the wealth constraint, and μ_t to be the date–t multiplier associated with the cash-in-advance constraint, the house-hold's efficiency conditions for this problem are:

(3.13)

(i) $1/c_t = \phi_t + \mu_t$ (consumption)

(ii) $\gamma = \phi_t(1 - \tau_{nt})w_t$ (labor supply)

(iii) $(\phi_t + \mu_t)/p_t = \beta\left[(\phi_{t+1} + \mu_{t+1})/p_{t+1}\right](1 + R_{t+1})$

   (bonds)

(iv) $\phi_t = \beta\left[\phi_{t+1}(1 - \delta(1 - \tau_{kt+1}) + (1 - \tau_{kt+1})r_{t+1})\right]$

   (capital)

(v) $\phi_t/p_t = \beta\left[(\phi_{t+1} + \mu_{t+1})/p_{t+1}\right]$ (money)

These first order conditions, with Equations 3.5, 3.6, 3.7, the competitive pricing condition, $B_{t+1} = b_{t+1}$, $K_{t+1} = k_{t+1}$, $M_{t+1} = m_t$, and $n_t = N_t$ characterize the competitive equilibrium of this economy. Since this is an economy distorted with money and taxes, the equilibrium cannot be backed out by solving a social planner's (optimization) problem, as in Kydland and Prescott (1982). Instead, I solve for an equilibrium directly using numerical methods.

Solving for a competitive equilibrium in this economy is a two-part process, and proceeds as follows. Recall that beginning with the second period in state ψ_2, which is the absorbing postwar state, money is withdrawn from the economy at a constant rate for N periods. I use a version of

Marcet's (1989) procedure to approximate the equilibrium during the transition from the second period in state ψ_2 to the new steady state. I choose to begin this approximation in period 2 of the absorbing state rather than in the first postwar period because the rate of money withdrawal in the first postwar period differs from subsequent periods, and would therefore entail the use of additional state variables. For example, assuming constant technology, tax rates, government spending, and money stock, and imposing equilibrium conditions, this approximation could be accomplished with Marcet's technique by simply parameterizing the Euler equations as functions of the aggregate capital stock. The complicating factor, however, is the temporary postwar policy of withdrawing money from the economy such that in the new steady state, the price level returns to its prewar value.

Beginning with period 2, this can be accommodated, however, by simply expanding the state vector to include (1) the money stock (M_t), (2) a state variable that indicates the constant deflationary policy is in effect for periods 2 through $N + 1$ of postwar peace, and (3) a state variable that indicates the number of remaining periods that the deflationary policy will be in place. Given the constant rate of money withdrawal during periods 2 through $N + 1$, we can define a variable m_g to indicate that the deflationary policy is in effect. (3) is simply an integer equal to the number of remaining periods that the deflationary policy will be in place, and is zero otherwise. This state variable is defined as d_p. Marcet's idea is to solve the expectational Euler equations of the problem by parameterizing them as arbitrary functions of current-dated state variables. In this case, the right hand sides of the three Euler equations 3.13 (iii-iv) are approximated as $H_1(S_2)$, $H_2(S_2)$, and $H_3(S_2)$, where H_i are arbitrary functions, and S_2 is the current state vector in the absorbing state.

Following Marcet (1989), I choose H_i to be a power function in the state variables.

This yields right-hand-sides of the Euler equations as power functions of state variables $(K_t, M_t, d_{pt}, m_{gt})$. In particular, first rearrange these equations:

(3.13.iii, iv. iv)

$$1 / (1 + R_{t+1}) = \beta \left[(\mu_{t+1} + \phi_{t+1}) / p_{t+1} \right] p_t / (\mu_t + \phi_t)$$

$$\phi_t = \beta \phi_{t+1} \left[1 - \delta (1 - \tau_{kt+1}) + (1 - \tau_{kt+1}) r_{t+1} \right]$$

$$1 / p_t = \beta \left[(\mu_{t+1} + \phi_{t+1} / p_{t+1} \right] / \phi_t$$

Next approximate these equations as power functions of the state variables:

$$1 / (1 + R_{t+1}) = A_0 K_t^{A_1} M_t^{A_2} dp_t^{A_3} m_{gt}^{A_4}$$

$$\phi_t = B_0 K_t^{B_1} M_t^{B_2} d_{pt}^{B_3} m_{gt}^{B_4}$$

$$1 / p_t = C_0 K_t^{C_1} M_t^{C_2} d_{pt}^{C_3} m_{gt}^{C_4}$$

and obtain estimates of the A_i, B_i and C_i by the iterative procedure outlined in Chapter 2. To obtain the equilibrium, set factor prices equal to their marginal products, which can be obtained from the estimates for ϕ_t. Next, use ϕ_t, the government budget constraint, and p_t to solve for consumption, and then back out μ_t. Next period's capital stock, k_{t+1} can be obtained from the household's budget constraint, and is equated to the aggregate capital stock. I found this procedure to be very accurate; the Euler equation errors along the transition path to the new steady state were virtually zero.

Given decision rules to the household's problem in the absorbing state beginning with Period 2, step two is to solve the model during World War II and the first postwar period. First, recall that the war ends in period T. Therefore, we have from the efficiency conditions for holding capital, money, and bonds:

$$\phi_{T+1} = \beta\left[\phi_{T+2}\{(1 - \tau_{kT+2} + \delta\tau_{kT+2})r_{T+2} + (1 - \delta)\}\right] \quad \text{and}$$

$$1/p_{T+1} = \beta\left[(\phi_{T+2} + \mu_{T+2})/(\phi_{T+1},p_{T+2})\right]$$

$$(\phi_{T+1} + \mu_{T+1})/p_{T+1}) = \beta\left[(\phi_{T+2} + \mu_{T+2})/p_{T+2}\right](1 + R_{T+2})$$

Note that these three efficiency conditions are functions of ϕ_{T+2}, p_{T+2}, μ_{T+2} and r_{T+2} (and parameters), where $T + 2$ is the second postwar period. However, p_{T+2} and ϕ_{T+2} are given by the approximating functions for the absorbing state beginning at $T + 2$, and both r_{T+2} and μ_{T+2} are implicit functions of S_{2T+2}.

Given the initial conditions m_0, k_0, and b_0, there are $11(T + 1)$ unknowns:
$\{c_t\}_1^{T+1}$, $\{b_t\}_2^{T+2}$, $\{k_t\}_2^{T+2}$, $\{m_t\}_2^{T+2}$, $\{n_t\}_1^{T+1}$, $\{p_t\}_1^{T+1}$, $\{R_t\}_2^{T+2}$,
$\{\mu_t\}_1^{T+1}$ $\{\phi_t\}_1^{T+1}$, $\{r_t\}_1^{T+1}$, and $\{w_t\}_1^{T+1}$, (consumption, bonds, capital, money, labor input, prices, interest rates, CIA and budget multipliers, and factor prices) to solve for in $11(T + 1)$ nonlinear equations (First order conditions for consumption, money, bonds, capital, effort, firm efficiency conditions, the CIA constraint, the household budget con-

straint, the government budget constraint and the money market equilibrium condition).

The next step is to solve these $11(T + 1)$ nonlinear equations numerically. It is straightforward to verify that the solution to this set of equations, given the approximating functions for the absorbing state, characterizes the competitive equilibrium of this economy.

It is important to emphasize that these decision rules take as given that the government follows a postwar deflationary monetary policy similar to postwar policies followed in earlier war episodes.

3.4.2 *The Model with Temporary Price Controls*

Next, I consider the household's problem when the economy is subject to general price controls during the war.

For the postwar period, prices are not controlled, and the solution procedure for the absorbing state is identical to the method for this state described above. The war-time economy is modeled as a variant of the disequilibrium strategies advanced by Barro and Grossman, Benassy, Grandmont, and others. To solve the household's problem during the war, the first step is to fix nominal prices below the market clearing level for each period during the war episode. The specific way in which prices are set is discussed in Section 3.5.

With prices exogenously set, however, some of the efficiency conditions typically will not be satisfied. In particular, imposing maximum prices that are set below market clearing results in an excess demand situation in which households' first order condition for consumption does not generally hold. In this case, $u_{ct} \geq (\phi_t + \mu_t)\bar{p}_t$, where $\bar{p}_t$ is strictly less than the market clearing price. This inequality shows that household's would like to buy more than is offered.

Given that same efficiency condition will not hold, approximating the equilibrium can be difficult in this setup. To facilitate solving for the equilibrium, I adjust the model such that the household's marginal condition for consumption will be satisfied. I assume that with prices fixed below equilibrium, individuals can no longer acquire goods just with pre-accumulated cash, but also must expend leisure to acquire goods. This is intended to capture some of the effects of excess demand environments in which individuals queue to obtain goods selling at prices fixed below market clearing, or search for shops that have not run out of supplies, or make transactions on the black market.

In the spirit of the price control/rationing program that was in place during the war, I give households the right to purchase κ_t units of the consumption good in period t at the controlled price $\bar{p}_t$ Further purchases of the consumption good are bought on the black market at the market clearing price p_t^b. In addition to the CIA constraint, shopping time is required to purchase goods by assuming that $F(n^2) \geq$ consumption, where n^2 is time spent transacting, $F: \Re^+ \Rightarrow \Re^+$, and F is assumed to be continuous and concave. For simplicity, I assume that the same technology is used to acquire both rationed goods at the controlled price and goods on the black market. Following Evans (1982), I also assume that a market exists for trading coupons (κ_t), with a competitive price $\hat{p}_t$. Since the technology for acquiring goods in the black market is the same as in the controlled market, it follows that in equilibrium, $\hat{p}_t = p_t^b - \bar{p}_t$. Given the price and rationing controls for consumers, it is necessary to impose some restrictions on firms. It is assumed that firms must supply up to κ_t units of the consumption good at the controlled price $\bar{p}_t$, given that a consumer has sufficient cash and coupons, and has expended the required amount of time. The amount sold at the controlled price is denoted as c_{1t}, with $c_{1t} \leq \kappa_t$. In addition, the government can also purchase the good at the controlled price with available cash:

$$(M_{t+1} - M_t) + B_{t+1} - (1 + R_t) B_t$$

This results in negative profits, π_t, which are borne by the owners of the firm (households):

$$\pi_t = \lambda_t K_t^{\theta}, N_t^{1-\theta} - w_t N_t - r_t K_t + c_{1t} (\bar{p}_t - p_t^b) / p_t^b -$$

$$(1 / \bar{p}_t - 1 / p_t^b) + [(m_{t+1} - m_t) + B_{t+1} - (1 + R_t) B_t].$$

In addition to these changes, we also have the following modification of the household's problem. In Hansen's (1985) indivisible labor economy, preferences were of the form $\log(c)t + v(l_t)$, where $l_t = 1 - \bar{h}$ or $l_t = 1$, and $\bar{h}$ is full-time hours. With employment lotteries and separable utility between consumption and leisure, the equilibrium consumption allocation is independent of employment status, and date t expected utility for the representative household reduces to $\log(c_t) + \alpha_t v(1 - \bar{h}) + (1 - \alpha_t) v(1)$, where α_t is the date t probability of working. This can be rearranged to deliver linear utility in leisure for the representative household.

Now, with time spent acquiring goods in the indivisible labor economy, $\text{leisure}_{wt} = 1 - \bar{h} - n_{wt}^2$, or $\text{leisure}_{nwt} = 1 - n_{nwt}^2$, depending on the employment status, w = working, nw = not working, with $n^2 \equiv$ time spent transacting. Even with separable utility across consumption and leisure, and lotteries, consumption in the employed and unemployed states will no longer be identical. Utility for employed households is given by: $\log(c_w) + v(1 - h - n_w^2)$, while utility for the unemployed is: $\log(c_{nw}) + v(1 - n_{nw}^2)$.

For comparative and computational purposes, it is convenient to maintain Hansen's original setup of a representative agent that has preferences defined linearly over leisure. To maintain the representative household construct, I approximate the household's preferences as:

$$\log(c_{it}) + v^1(1 - h_{it}) - v^2(n_{it}^2),$$

where v^2 is an increasing and convex function. With this approximation, utility is separable across c, h, and n^2, and this allows me to retain the representative agent construct with consumption allocations that are independent of the employment status. Expected utility for the representative agent becomes: $\log(c_t) + \alpha_t v^1(1 - h_t) - v^2(n_t^2)$. In practice, I will *choose* this function to be quadratic: $v(n^2) = \zeta_1 n^2 + \zeta(n^2)^2$. The parameters ζ_1 and ζ_2 are calculated from a Taylor-series expansion around the original utility function:

$$\log(1 - h - n^2) \cong \log(1 - h) - \zeta_1 n^2 - \zeta_2(n^2)^2,$$

where $\zeta_1 = (1/1 - h)$ and $\zeta_2 = (1/1 - h)^2$, and h is evaluated at the steady state for the representative household. Given this approximation and the modified constraints, the representative household's problem becomes:

$$\text{Max} \sum_{t=0}^{\infty} \beta^t \left[\log(c_{1t} + c_{2t}) - \gamma n_{1t} - \zeta_1 n_{2t} - \zeta^2 (n_{2t})^2 \right]$$

subject to:

(A)

$$m_t + p_t^b TR_t + (1 + R_t) b_t +$$

$$p_t^b (1 - \tau_{nt}) w_t n_{1t} + p_t^b (1 - \tau_{kt}) r_t k_t + p_t^b \delta \tau_{kt} k_t +$$

$$\hat{p} \kappa_t^8 + p_t^b (1 - \delta) k_t - \hat{p} \kappa_t^d - \bar{p}_t c_{1t} -$$

$$p_t^b c_{2t} - m_{t+1} - p_t^b k_{t+1} - b_{t+1} + \pi_t \geq 0$$

(B)

$$m_t + (1 + R_t) b_t + \hat{p} \kappa_t^8 - \hat{p} \kappa_t^d - b_{t+1} - Bl_t - Cu_t \geq 0$$

(C) $$Cu_t - \bar{p}_t c_{1t} \geq 0$$

(D) $$Bl_t - p_t^b c_{2t} \geq 0$$

(E) $$F(n_t^2) - c_{1t} - c_{2t} \geq 0$$

(F) $\qquad$ $\kappa_t^d - c_{1t} \geq 0$

and the governments period budget constraint is:

$$g_t + (1 + R_t)B_t / \bar{p}_t =$$

$$B_{t+1} / \bar{p}_t + \tau_{nt} w_t N_t^1 + \tau_{kt}(r_t - \delta)K_t + (M_{t+1} - M_t)/\bar{p}_t$$

Note that for the government, the relevant price is the controlled price since by assumption the government purchases goods at that price.

The efficiency conditions during the war are (subscripts indicate partial derivatives):

(3.14)

(i) $\quad 1/(c_{1t} + c_{2t}) = \bar{p}_t \phi_t + \bar{p}_t \mu_{1t} + \psi_{1t} + \psi_{2t}$ (Rationed Goods)

(ii) $\quad 1/(c_{1t} + c_{2t}) = p_t^b \phi_t + p_t^b \mu_{2t} + \psi_{1t}$ (Black Market Goods)

(iii) $\quad \gamma = p_t^b \phi_t (1 - \tau_{nt}) w_t$ (labor input–production)

(iv) $\quad \zeta_1 + 2\zeta_2 n_{2t} = \psi_{1t} F_{n2t}$ (labor input–shopping)

(v) $\quad \mu_{2t} = \mu_t$ (currency choice for black market)

(vi) $\quad \mu_{1t} = \mu_t$ (currency choice for rationed goods)

(vii) $\quad p_t^b \phi_t = p_{t+1}^b \left[\phi_{t+1} (1 - \tau_{ktn}) r_{t+1} + \delta \tau_{kt+1} \right]$ (next period capital stock)

(viii) $\phi_t + \mu_t = \beta(\phi_{t+1} + \mu_{t+1})(r_{t+1} + 1)$ (next period bonds)

(ix) $\beta V_{mt+1} = \phi$ (next period money holdings)

(x) $\hat{p}_t(\phi_t + \mu_t) = \psi_{2t}$ (choice of coupons),

the constraints holding at equality, and the transversality conditions.

 The modified CIA constraints are given by (B) and (C), and (E). (B) states that initial wealth (in dollars) for asset market trading is given by $m + (1 + R)b + \hat{p}\kappa$, and this is used to acquire new debt (b'), cash for black market trading (*Bl*), coupons for the rationed good ($\hat{p}\kappa^d$), and sufficient cash to purchase κ^d units of the rationed good at the controlled price ($\bar{p}_t$). As described above, the shopping constraint $F(n_2) \geq (c_1 + c_2)$ is included to capture some of the inefficiencies created by price controls. This yields the modified choice condition

$$1 / (c_1 + c_2) = (\phi p^b + \mu_2 p^b + \psi_2),$$

where ψ_2 is the multiplier associated with the shopping constraint. Note that $p^b \geq \bar{p}$,, and if $p^b = \bar{p}$, then the constraint on sales of the coupon good does not bind, and both ψ^2 and $\hat{p}$ are zero.

 A solution can be obtained for this constrained war-time economy under price controls by using the technique developed for the flexible-price war-time economy.

3.5 CALIBRATING THE MODEL
WITH PRICE CONTROLS

To obtain the solution to this economy, we need to assign values to the new components of the model: $\{M_t\}$, $\{\bar{p}_t\}$, $F(n^2)$, $\{\kappa_t\}$. As noted above, F is assumed to be identical for both legal purchases and black market activity. Since total consumption is comprised of both legal and black market purchases, and the same shopping technology is assumed for both types of purchases, we have considerable freedom in choosing $\{\kappa_t\}$. Total consumption chosen by the household in equilibrium, however, will be affected by the shopping function $F(n^2)$.

For simplicity, I assume that F is linear: $F(n^2) = A n^2$. The technology parameter A will determine the fraction of time households spend in acquiring consumption. I have been unable to find explicit estimates of the additional amount of time required for shopping during World War II as a result of price controls, but it does not appear to have been substantial. Therefore, I choose A such that households on average spend about two percent of their time endowment shopping during the war. This is comparable to figures referenced by Rockoff (1984). Second, it is necessary to choose the sequence of controlled prices, $\{p_t\}$. I choose $\{p_t\}$ to approximate reported price increases over the course of the war. Given that the Office of Price Administration froze prices in March 1942, which is roughly the second quarter of U.S. participation in the war, I use the market clearing price level for the first period of the war. The average reported inflation rate over the course of the war is then used to fix the reported price level over the remainder of the war.

It is also difficult to obtain direct evidence on $\{\kappa_t\}$, which is the amount of consumption the representative household

can obtain with its coupon issue at the controlled price. Given
our assumptions regarding the transactions technology and
the black market, the choice of $\{\kappa_t\}$ is not central for
determination of equilibrium. Rockoff (1984) reports that
issue of ration coupons rose over the course of the war, so κ_1
is set equal to 70 percent of steady state consumption, and κ_T
is 80 percent of the steady state level.

The $\{M_t\}$ sequence is set to match the behavior of M1
over the course of World War II. The average annual growth
rate of M1 during World War II was 18 percent, and this
growth rate is used to generate the World War II money
stock. For this experiment, the postwar money sequence is
calibrated to approximate earlier postwar monetary policies.
The most striking feature of these historical policies is that
despite the rapid increase in the money stock during the war,
the postwar price level approximately returns to its prewar
value. To construct this policy, the first step is to make a
guess for the steady state of the postwar economy. This guess
and the restriction that the steady state postwar price level
equals its prewar level pins down the steady state money
stock.

For the transition from the wartime money stock to the
steady state money stock, money is set for the first period
after the war such that the price level is approximately
unchanged from the last war period. Starting in the second
postwar period, money is then withdrawn at a constant rate
for N periods. The rate of withdrawal (m_g) is set at the
maximum rate such that the CIA constraint still binds. N is
then pinned down as the required number of periods of
reducing the money stock at rate m_g to achieve the new
asymptotic money stock such that the new steady state price
level is equal to the old steady state level. Capital and Labor
income tax rates, and government spending and technology

shocks during the war are taken from the previous chapter. Postwar technology is normalized to one for all t, and government spending is fixed at its unconditional mean.

The values of the other parameters in the model are taken from the calibration in Chapter 2.

3.6 ECONOMIC ANALYSIS OF MONETARY POLICIES

The distortion resulting from price controls, which is that individuals now must expend leisure, as well as cash to acquire consumption goods, results in lower labor supply, lower consumption, a lower capital stock, and consequently, higher public debt. Labor input in the controlled economy is about seven percent lower than in the market clearing model at the end of the war. Similarly, output in the controlled economy is about five percent lower than in the market clearing model. It is interesting to note that these results are similar to those calculated by Evans (1982) who used a very different framework.

These results, however, are somewhat surprising, given that the distortions from price controls in this model are relatively small. For example, the same shopping technology was used for acquiring both legal rationed goods and black market goods, and this shopping function was calibrated to be relatively productive; at the peak of the war, households spend about three additional hours per week shopping. Given the legal penalties for black market trading during World War II, it seems reasonable to assume that the costs of black market transactions exceeded those presented here. Moreover, this problem was constructed so that households were always able to purchase as much consumption as desired, provided that they spent the required amount of time. Shortages of several goods developed over the course of the war, however, including gasoline, automobiles and other consumer durables, and some foodstuffs. Incorporating higher costs of controls and binding rationing constraints would certainly result in lower labor supply during the war in this model economy. Given that the costs of controls and rationing may be significantly understated in this analysis, it is somewhat puzzling why labor input rose so dramatically during World War II.

The next experiment analyzes the economic effects of the high inflation that occurred immediately after World War II. As noted earlier, I assume that households believe with certainty that the government will adopt the kind of deflationary policy pursued after earlier U.S. wars. Accordingly, the inflation that emerges after World War II is entirely unexpected.

First, it is useful to examine more closely the time path of money over the war and the immediate postwar period, and explore the extent to which post-World War II monetary policy differed relative to earlier postwar polices. Balke and Gordon (1986) report a value of M1 that roughly doubles over the course of World War II. Virtually identical behavior is reported for other monetary aggregates such as M2 and the Monetary Base. Immediately following the end of the war, all three of these aggregates continued to grow at about five percent per year, while real GNP declined to nearly its prewar value by 1946. For example, the output-money ratio, with money measured as M1, was about 9 at the beginning of World War II, but falls to 4.5 by 1947. It is interesting to contrast this behavior to the World War I experience, in which the output-money ratio is about 12 at the start of World War I, and is about 11 after the 1920-21 deflation. Post-World

War II monetary policy differed considerably from earlier postwar episodes.

At the end of the war, the ratio of nominal public debt to nominal GNP stood at about 1.2, while nominal prices rose about 60 percent between 1945 and 1948. These data suggest that inflation eliminated public debt equal to about 40 percent of GNP. This increase overstates the true reduction in the value of the public debt to the extent that measured prices during World War II differed from true transactions prices. For example, if some wartime transactions take place at prices higher than maximum legal prices, then a price level based on controlled prices would be artificially low. In addition, the quality of goods supplied may decline as a result of price controls, which implies that wartime and postwar consumption bundles differ.

For this experiment, the rate of inflation determines the extent to which the public debt is repudiated, and therefore is a key parameter. Rather than use the published price level statistics from World War II, I simply use the model economy to calculate the immediate postwar inflation. This consists of a two-part process. First, I solve for the equilibrium over the course of the war, conditional on the assumption that households believe with certainty that the government will follow a deflationary policy after World War II similar to historical postwar monetary policies. This provides a sequence of price levels over the course of the war. Once the war ends, the government, however, does not follow the historical policy of deflating back to the prewar price level. Instead, I assume that the money stock remains permanently at its end-of-war level. In addition, tax rates are adjusted such that present value budget balance is achieved, and there are no further disturbances to government spending or production possibilities. Solving for the perfect foresight equilibrium to this stationary, postwar economy yields a sequence of postwar price level, and the immediate postwar inflation can then be calculated.

Equilibrium allocations obtained under the surprise inflation can then be compared to allocations under the counterfactual policy of deflating after wars.

Rather than a 60 percent increase in the postwar price level, I find that the price level rises about 30 percent. While the steady state price level differs between this economy and the economy under counterfactual experiment of deflating back to the prewar price level, note that both economies have zero inflation in the steady state.

The historical deflationary policy has two important effects. First, by returning the price level to its prewar level, the real value of the World War II debt is higher, and thus requires higher taxes on factor incomes to achieve present value budget balance. Second, money must be withdrawn from the economy such that the new steady state price level coincides with the prewar price level. I assume that the government must issue new debt to withdraw this wartime currency from the economy. This additional debt must then be paid off, which requires higher distorting taxes on factor incomes.

I find that constant tax rates of about 25 percent on labor income and 54 percent on capital income are required to obtain present value budget balance at the end of 2000 periods under the historical deflationary policy, and rates of about 24 percent on labor income and 51 percent on capital income in the case of not deflating.

Abstracting from time consistency/reputational issues, the decision of the government to deviate from historical deflationary policies has important long-run implications for the U.S. economy. Figure 17 presents the transition of the capital stock following the war to its postwar steady state under the counterfactual of the historical deflationary policy, and also the actual policy of not deflating. Note that the steady state capital stock under the deflationary policy is nearly eight percent lower than under the policy of not deflating, which is equivalent to about 1 trillion current dollars. Figure 18 presents the transition path of period utility to the new steady state for both of these economies. Note that steady state utility for the representative household would be about three percent lower if the traditional deflationary policy had been followed. Figure 19 presents the transition path of labor supply in these two economies. In the steady state, labor input is about two percent higher in the case of not deflating. Figure 20 presents the transition path of consumption to the postwar steady state for the two economies. Higher labor and capital inputs support higher consumption of about 4.5 percent; this is equivalent to about $200 billion per year. The transition path of output is presented in Figure 21, and the steady state under the deflationary policy is about four percent lower than under the actual policy. This is equivalent to about $250 billion per year.

Figure 22 presents the transition path of the price level for these two economies. Under the counterfactual deflationary policy, the price level returns to its prewar steady state value. Under the constant money (actual) policy, the new steady state price level is nearly twice the prewar steady state price level.

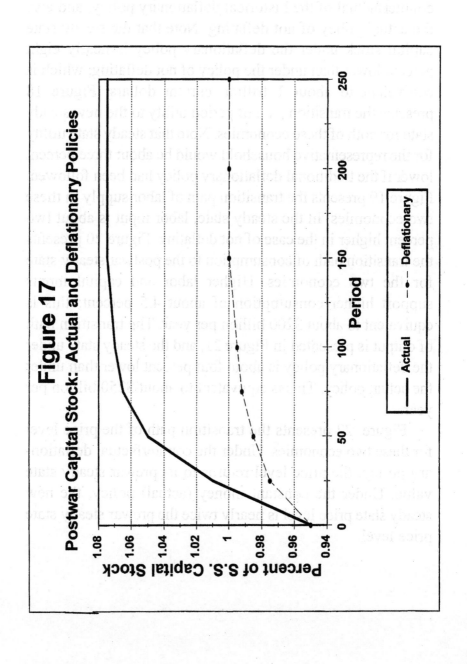

Figure 17

Postwar Capital Stock: Actual and Deflationary Policies

Figure 18

Postwar Utility: Actual and Deflationary Policies

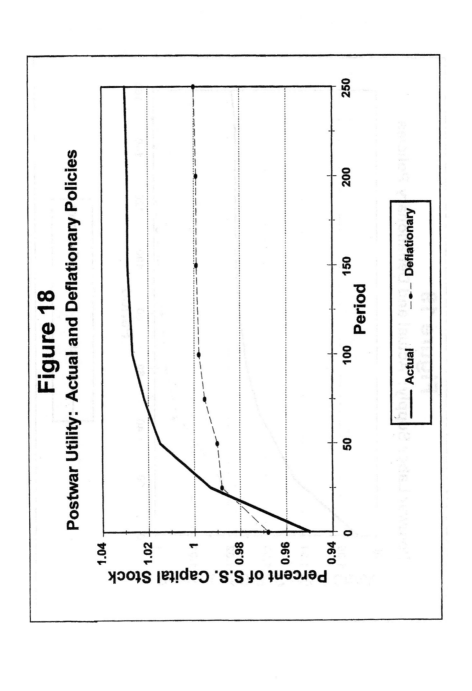

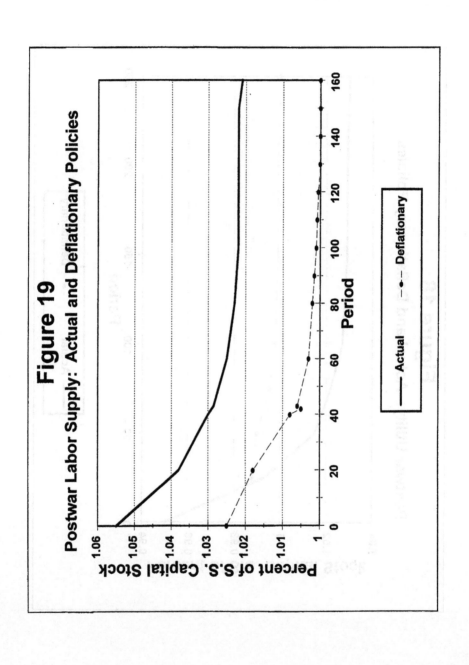

Figure 19

Postwar Labor Supply: Actual and Deflationary Policies

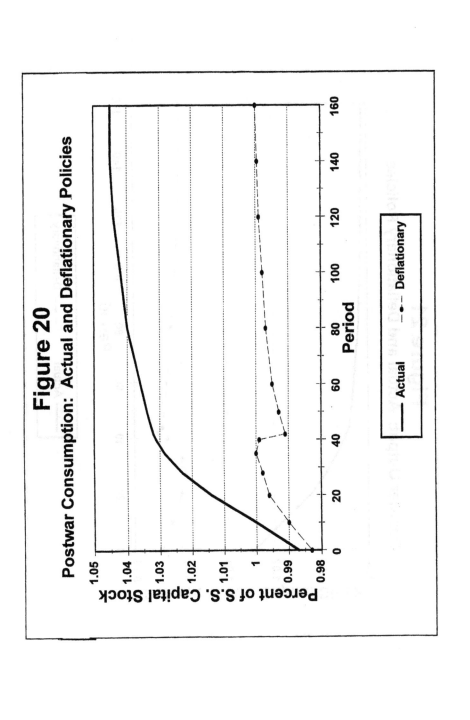

Figure 20

Postwar Consumption: Actual and Deflationary Policies

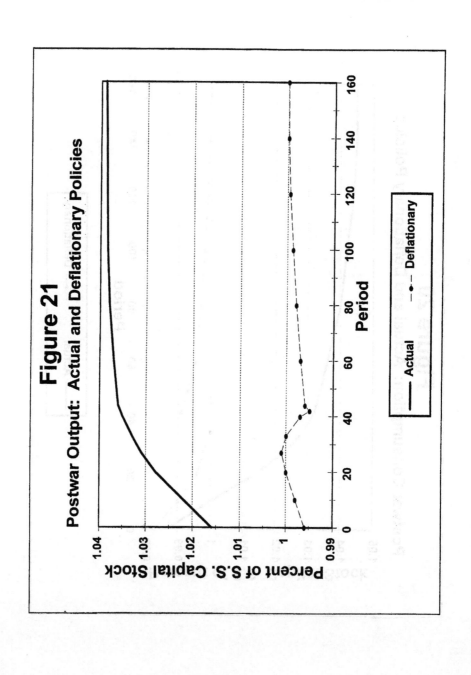

Figure 21

Postwar Output: Actual and Deflationary Policies

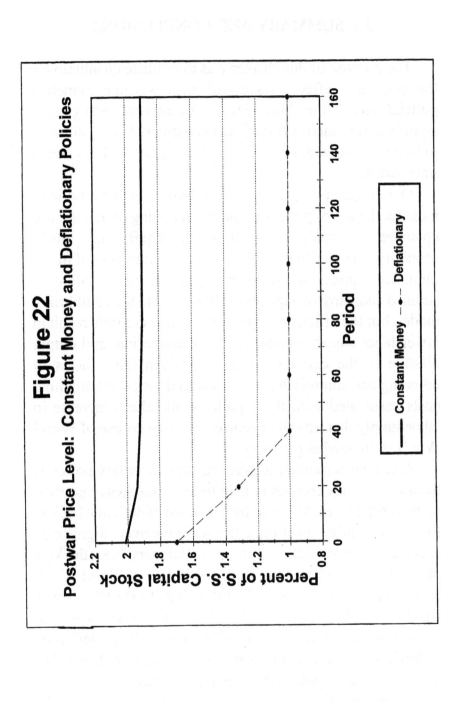

Figure 22

Postwar Price Level: Constant Money and Deflationary Policies

3.7 SUMMARY AND CONCLUSIONS

The purpose of this chapter was to evaluate quantitatively the economic effects associated with wartime monetary policies used in the United States. An intertemporal general equilibrium monetary model was constructed and calibrated to be consistent with key features of aggregate U.S. economic time series.

One important feature of wartime monetary policies includes the use of price controls and rationing during the war episodes. To study this feature, the equilibrium model economy was modified to allow for the imposition of maximum legal prices and rationing. The behavior of the constrained economy was qualitatively similar to the equilibrium model, but the efficiency losses from price controls result in lower labor supply, capital stock, consumption, and output relative to the equilibrium model. Given the policies of rationing and controls during the war and the potentially high costs associated with these policies, the sharp increase in labor supply that actually occurred over the course of World War II is somewhat puzzling.

A second important feature wartime monetary policy is the use of money creation to help finance emergency government expenditures, followed by a practice of deflation back to the prewar price level once the war was over. Significant postwar deflations followed the Revolutionary War, the War of 1812, the Mexican War, the Civil War, and World War I. Monetary policy immediately following World War II was strikingly different relative to these other episodes in that there was a substantial inflation, rather than deflation, following the end of the war. This surprise inflation has important positive and normative implications for the postwar U.S. economy. If the historical policy of deflating back to the prewar price level had been followed, higher capital and labor income taxes would have been required to pay off the additional debt. As a result, I estimate that the capital stock would permanently be eight percent lower, and consumption and output about four percent lower. Moreover, utility would be about 3 percent lower, and to compensate individuals would be an increase of about 3 percent permanently higher consumption.

From a normative perspective, monetary policy immediately following World War II represents one of the most important shifts in government policy in the history of the United States. Perhaps not coincidentally, this inflationary episode ushered in the postwar U.S. policy of persistent inflation that has continued over the past 50 years.

Table 4

Welfare Costs of Alternative Monetary Policies

Policy	τ_n	τ_k	Relative Cost of War Policies
Surprise Inflation	.237	.510	0.0%
Standard Postwar Deflationary Policy	.256	.554	3.0%

Appendix A

Solution Technique

This appendix presents the technique used to solve for the competitive equilibrium in the economies considered in this paper. For a more detailed description of the method of parameterizing expectations, see Marcet (1988), and Marshall and Marcet (1992).

The technique applied in this paper uses an extension of Marcet's idea of parameterizing expectations. For example, consider the Brock-Mirman growth model with a stationary first-order Markov process for technology. The intertemporal efficiency condition, consumption governing today vs. consumption tomorrow is given by

$$(1) \qquad u_{c,t} = \beta E_{t+1}[u_{ct+1}(F_{kt+1}) + (1 - \delta)],$$

where u_c is marginal utility of consumption, and F_k is the marginal product of capital. Marcet's idea is to approximate the right-hand side of (1) with a function of the state variables $\psi(s, \gamma)$. The state vector is denoted s, which for this example includes the current capital stock (k_t) and the current technology (λ_t), and γ is a parameter vector. We can write s as: $s_t = f(s_{t-1}, \gamma, \epsilon_t)$. Marcet suggests using an approximating function belonging to the family of polynomials. In this case, if (1) is a continuous function of λ, the Stone-Wierstrass theorem implies that the function can approximate the right-hand side arbitrarily well for a sufficiently large number of polynomial terms.

To calculate values of the polynomial coefficients γ, Marcet suggests using an interactive nonlinear least squares routine. For the Brock-Morman model, the steps are:

(1) Generate $\{\lambda\}_1^{T+1}$, choose k_0 and other initial conditions.

(2) Choose ψ from the family of polynomials. In practice, exponential polynomials of the form

$$\psi = \exp \log(\gamma_0) + \sum_{i=1}^{n} \gamma_i \log(s_i) + \sum_{i=1}^{n} \sum_{k=1}^{n} \gamma_{ik} \log(s_i) * \log(s_k) + ...)$$

work well for this type of model.

(3) Given the polynomial approximating function of order ν, choose initial values for the ν–dimensional parameter vector γ, and denote this as γ^1.

(4) Calculate $u_{c,t} = \psi(s, \gamma^1) \rightarrow k_{t+1} = k(\psi(s, \gamma^1))$.

(5) Calculate

$$\hat{B} = \operatorname{argmin} 1/T \sum_1^T (u_{c,t+1}(s_{t+1}, \gamma^1) F_{k,t+1}(s_{t+1}, \gamma^1) + (1 - \delta) - \psi(s_t, \hat{\gamma}))^2$$

(6) Update β as $\gamma^2 = \theta\hat{\gamma} + (1 - \theta)\gamma^1, \quad \theta \in (0,1]$.

(7) Repeat over i until $\max_j |\gamma_t^{i+1} - \gamma_j^i| < \tau$ where γ_j is the j-element of γ, and τ is a tolerance level.

For $\gamma \in B$, where B is the space of ν–dimension parameter vectors,

$$\gamma^* = \operatorname*{argmin}_{\gamma \in B} 1/T \sum_1^T \left(u_{c,t+1}(s_{t+1}, b) F_{k,t+1}(s_{t+1}, b) + (1 - \delta) - \psi(s_t, b) \right)^2$$

Note that in this Brock–Mirman setup, the polynomial coefficients γ can be solved for using a long simulation. Thus, this approach to solving dynamic, stochastic, nonlinear models is a version of Monte Carlo integration.

For the economies considered in this paper, however, it is difficult to obtain good estimates of the polynomial coefficients by using a single, long simulation. This is because the economies that we consider experience World War II and the Korean War just once before reaching the absorbing peace state ψ_s. In this case, there are very few observations for calculating the polynomial coefficients for the state variables that describe the two war episodes.

Instead, I use simulations based on a "cross-section" of economies. This approach has been used by Marcet and Marimon (1990) and Marshall (1992). The basic idea is to generate M independent and identically distributed shock processes. Thus, we generate M i.i.d. technology shocks of length T+1 , M i.i.d. government spending shocks of length M i.i.d. durations of World War II, M i.i.d. durations of the Korean War, M i.i.d. start dates for World War II, and M i.i.d. start dates for the Korean War. This allows us to generate M different realizations of this economy. The approximating function is then obtained by estimating the nonlinear regressions as a panel, consisting of MT observations. Consistency can be proven for large M, holding T fixed. [See Marcet and Marshall (1992)]. The specific solution technique for this application can be described as follows:

1. Choose M and T. I fix $M = 25$, and $T = 650$.
    For each $m \in M$:

    (A) Specify parameters and initial capital stock. The initial capital stock is set at the deterministic

steady state. Draw technology shocks and government spending shocks over the entire horizon of
the economy, which is length $T + 1$. These shocks
are generated only once per economy. Draw a
starting date for World War II. Draw the duration
of World War II. Draw a starting date for the
Korean War. Draw the duration of the Korean
War. Given the war/peace states and government
spending shocks, the sequence of government
spending of length $T + 1(\{g_t\}_1^{T+1})$ can be calculated. Given the war/peace states, the sequences of
labor and capital tax rates $(\{\tau_{nt}\}_1^{T+1}, \{\tau_{kt}\}_1^{T+1})$ can
be calculated.

(B) Approximate the conditional expectations in the
first order conditions as functions of the relevant
state variables. In this application, I use first order
power functions:

$$(1/1 + R) = A_0 \lambda^{A_1} K^{A_2} g^{A_3} d_w^{A_4} d_k^{A_5} \{\Pi_2^5 (\psi_i^{A_{i+4}})\}$$

$$\phi = B_0 \lambda^{B_1} K^{B_2} g^{B_3} d_w^{B_4} d_k^{B_5} \{\Pi_2^5 (\psi_i^{B_{i+4}})\},$$

where ϕ is the marginal value of wealth, g is
government spending, d_w is duration of World
War II, given that the state is ψ_2 and d_k is the
duration of the Korean War, given that the state is ψ_4.
Marcet (1989) has suggested the use of power
functions in approximating these conditional
expectations, and Den Haan and Marcet (1990)
have found that first order power functions work
well.

(C) Given initial estimates for the parameters of the approximating polynomials, the two parameterized Euler equations can be used to generate initial values for consumption and the interest rate.

(D) Given the initial guess for consumption, use the efficiency conditions for the firm and the household's intratemporal efficiency condition to solve for labor supply, the wage rate and the rental rate of capital.

(E) Given B_t, use the government's period budget constraint to solve for B_{t+1}. Substituting B_{t+1} into the household's budget constraint, K_{t+1} follows immediately.

(F) Repeat steps (A) – (E) over the remaining horizon. This yields an economy with $T + 1$ "observations."

2. Update the parameters of the approximating functions using the generated data. For the M economies, estimate as a panel the following nonlinear equations:

$$z_1 = A_0 \lambda^{A_1} K^{A_2} g^{A_3} d_w^{A_4} d_k^{A_5} \{ \Pi_2^5 (\psi_i^{A_{i+4}}) \} + \epsilon_1$$

$$z_2 = B_0 \lambda^{B_1} K^{B_2} g^{B_3} d_w^{B_4} d_k^{B_5} \{ \Pi_2^5 (\psi_i^{B_{i+4}}) \} + \epsilon$$

where z_i is the actual right-hand side of the relevant Euler equation. These equations are estimated by fitting a linear regression on the first-order Taylor series expansion of the approximating function. Next, update the approximating parameters via the scheme $B' = \theta S(B) + (1 - \theta)B$, $\theta \in (0,1]$, where B is the parameter used to generate the most recent data, and $S(B)$ is from the nonlinear regression fit to that data. Repeat (A) – (F), and continue this procedure until B converges to $S(B)$. In this application I chose four digits of accuracy for convergence to the fixed point $S(B)$.

I also compared the results from this method to the results from the procedure of first solving for the stationary state 5 allocations, and then working backwards to solve for decision rules in the other states. (I also used the method of parameterizing expectations for this approach). I found that the difference between these two techniques was generally less than one percent. Based on these results, I concluded that the method used in this paper was reasonable.

Appendix B

Model Calibration

$\beta = 0.99$ Household discount factor.

$\gamma = 2.11$ Leisure Preference Parameter for Representative Household

$\theta = 0.36$ Capital's Share of Income

$\delta = 0.175$ Quarterly Depreciation Rate of Capital

$\rho_\lambda = 0.95$ Autoregressive Parameter for Technology.

$\sigma_{\epsilon\lambda} = 0.0076$ Standard Deviation of Technology Shock.

v_g = 12% of Steady State Output for states 1 and 5—Government Spending.

v_g = mean of deviations from trend for states 2–4; Government Spending.

$\rho_g = 0.93$ Autoregressive Parameter for Government Spending Shock.

$\sigma_{\epsilon g} = 0.027$ Standard Deviation of Government Spending Shock.

τ_n (postwar average) = Marginal Labor Tax Rate from Joines (1981)

τ_k (postwar average) = .50; Marginal Labor Tax
                        Rate from Joines (1981)

Notes

1. In addition to Barro (1979), and Lucas and Stokey (1983), the optimal taxation literature includes work by Chamley (1981), Chari, Christiano, and Kehoe (1990), Judd (1989), King (1990), and Lucas (1990). Most of this work draws heavily on the early analysis of Ramsey (1927). Empirical investigations of optimal taxation include Barro (1981), Bizer and Durlauf (1990), and Sahasakul (1986).

2. Using a real business cycle model, Wynne (1990) finds that output rises significantly in response to temporary increases in government purchases, such as those that occurred during World War II.

3. While utility is linear in leisure for the representative household, this implication doesn't restrict intertemporal labor supply elasticity to infinite at the level of the individual household. The details of this model are presented in Hansen (1985). I investigate the sensitivity of this preference specification in Ohanian (1997). I find that balanced-budget policies are less distorting if utility is concave, rather than linear, in leisure.

4. In the environment analyzed in this book, I assume that net investment can be negative. This implies that capital can be consumed, or in an international context, capital can be sold for consumption. This assumption about investment provides a natural complement to the environment of non-negative investment which I analyzed in my 1997 *American Economic Review* paper. Qualitatively, the results are similar between the two cases. Quantitatively, the negative effects of

balanced-budget type policies are more pronounced in the model in which net investment can be negative. This is because constraining investment to be nonnegative effectively reduces the elasticity of investment.

5. Barro (1989) discusses how public expenditures may effect utility by substituting for private spending. He notes that while expenditures such as school lunch programs may be almost perfect substitutes for private spending, deployment of national defense provides very little substitution for private consumption. Alternatively, Baxter and King (1990) rationalize military purchases by allowing them to enter utility in an additively separable form, which does not alter private consumption decisions.

6. A number of techniques for solving nonlinear rational expectations models are described in the January 1990 issue of the *Journal of Business and Economic Statistics.*

7. Removing the trend using the Hodrick-Prescott procedure yields very similar results.

8. In Ohanian (1997), I conducted this exercise using a perfect foresight approach and no shocks to technology. The results were very similar.

9. The search for maximum tax revenue was conducted by starting at baseline tax rates of $\tau_n = .2$, and $\tau_k = .6$. First, I defined grids on labor and capital income. The labor tax grid was defined over [.2, .5], and the capital tax grid was defined over [.5, .9]. The initial distance between grid points was set at .05. Present value tax revenue was then calculated for each combination of capital tax rates and labor tax rates. This ex-

periment suggested a labor tax rate of .35 and capital tax rate of .85 for a maximum tax revenue. Next, I constructed a finer grid around these points to locate the rates used in the analysis of this chapter.

10. The calculations made by Lucas (1987) and those presented here, abstract from potential effects of stabilization on the *average* level of consumption. Greenwood and Huffman (1991) evaluate policies involving state contingent tax-subsidy schemes, and I find that they increase the mean level of output. It is not clear, however, that the removal of distortions achieved by these policies necessarily falls under the rubric of business cycle stabilization.

Bibliography

Balke, Nathan S. and Robert J. Gordon. Appendix B: Historical Data in *The American Business Cycle*. Robert J. Gordon, ed. Chicago: The University of Chicago Press, 1986.

Barro, Robert J. "The Neoclassical Approach to Fiscal Policy," in *Business Cycle Theory*. Robert J. Barro, ed. Cambridge: Harvard University Press, 1989.

Barro, Robert J. *Macroeconomics*. New York: Wiley, 1984.

Barro, Robert J. *On the Predictability of Tax Rate Changes*. Discussion Paper, University of Rochester, 1981.

Barro, Robert J. "On the Determination of the Public Debt," *Journal of Political Economy*, 87: 940-971, 1979.

Barro, Robert J. and Chaipat Sahasakul. "Average Marginal Tax Rates from Social Security and the Individual Income Tax, *Journal of Business*, 59: 555-566, 1981.

Barro, Robert J. and Herschel Grossman. *Money, Employment, and Inflation*. New York: Cambridge University Press, 1976.

Benassy, Jean P. *The Economics of Market Disequilibrium*. New York: Academic Press, 1982.

Bizer, David and Steven Durlauf. *Testing the Positive Theory of Government Finance*. Discussion Paper, Stanford University, Palo Alto, 1990.

Chamley, Christophe. "The Welfare Cost of Capital Income Taxation in a Growing Economy," *Journal of Political Economy*, 89: 468-496, 1981.

Chari, V.V., Lawrence Christiano, and Patrick Kehoe. *Optimal Fiscal and Monetary Policy: Some Recent Results*. Discussion Paper, Federal Reserve Bank of Minneapolis, Minneapolis, 1991.

Christiano, Lawrence. "Why Does Inventory Investment Fluctuate So Much?," *Journal of Monetary Economics*, 21: 247-280, 1988.

Cooley, Thomas F. and Gary Hansen. "The Inflation Tax in a Real Business Cycle Model," *American Economic Review*, 79: 733-748, 1989.

Cooley, Thomas F. and Gary Hansen. "Tax Distortions in a Neoclassical Monetary Economy," forthcoming, *Journal of Economic Theory*.

den Haan, Wouter J. "The Optimal Inflation Path in a Sidrauski–type Model with Uncertainty," *Journal of Monetary Economics*, 25, 389-410, 1990.

den Haan, Wouter J. and Albert Marcet. "Solving the Stochastic Growth Model by Parameterizing Expectations," *Journal of Business and Economic Statistics*, 8, 31-34, 1990.

Evans, Paul. "The Effects of General Price Controls During World War II," *Journal of Political Economy*, 90: 944-966, 1982.

Flinn, Mary. *The Role of Energy Price Shocks in a Real Business Cycle Model.* Discussion Paper, Michigan State University, Lansing, 1991.

Friedman, Milton and Anna J. Schwarz. *A Monetary History of the United States*. Princeton: Princeton University Press, 1963.

Goldin, Claudia. "War," in *Encyclopaedia of American Economic History*. Glen Porter, ed. New York: Random House, 1980.

Grandmont, J.M. "On Keynesian Temporary Equilibria," *Review of Economic Studies*, 43: 53-67, 1982.

Greenwood, Jeremy and Gregory Huffman. "Tax Analysis in a Real Business Cycle Model: On Measuring Harberger

Triangles and Okun Gaps," *Journal of Monetary Economics*, 27: 167-190, 1991.

Hamilton, Alexander. *Papers on Public Credit*. Reprinted: Washington, Government Printing Office, 1787.

Hansen, Gary. "Indivisible Labor and the Business Cycle," *Journal of Monetary Economics*, 16: 309-328, 1985.

Joines, Douglas. "Estimates of Effective Marginal Tax Rates on Factor Income," *Journal of Business*, 54: 191-226, 1981.

Judd, Kenneth. *Optimal Taxation in Dynamic Stochastic Economies: Theory and Evidence*. Discussion Paper, Hoover Institution, Palo Alto, 1990.

Kendrick, John. *Productivity Trends in the United States*, Princeton: Princeton University Press, 1961.

Keynes, John M. *How to Pay for the War, (1940), reprinted in The Collected Writings of John Maynard Kenyes.* Volume IX: 367-439. London: Macmillan, 1972.

King, Robert G. *Observable Implications of Dynamically Optimal Taxation*. Discussion Paper, University of Rochester, Rochester, 1990.

Kydland, Finn and Edward C. Prescott. "Time to Build and Aggregate Fluctuations," *Econometrica*, 50: 1345-1370, 1982.

Lucas, Robert E. *Models of Business Cycles*. Oxford: Basil Blackwell, 1987.

Lucas, Robert E. "Interest Rates and Currency Prices in a Two-Country World," *Journal of Monetary Economics*, 10: 335-360, 1982.

Lucas, Robert E. Commentary. New York Times, August 28, 1981.

Lucas, Robert E. and Nancy Stokey. "Optimal Fiscal and Monetary Policy in an Economy Without Capital," *Journal of Monetary Economics*, 12: 55-93, 1983.

Marcet, Albert. *Solution of Nonlinear Models by Parameterizing Expectations*. Discussion Paper, Carnegie Mellon University, Pittsburgh, 1989.

Marcet, Albert and Ramon Marimon. *Communication, Commitment, and Growth*. Discussion Paper, Universitat Pompeu Fabra, Barcelona, 1990.

Marcet, Albert and David Marshall. *Solving Nonlinear Models by Parameterizing Expectations: Convergence Results*. Discussion Paper No. 73. Graduate School of Management, Northwestern University, Evanston, 1992.

Marshall, David. *Inflation and Asset Returns in a Monetary Economy*. Discussion Paper. Northwestern University, Evanston, 1992.

Ohanian, Lee. "The Macroeconomic Effects of War Finance in the United States: World War II and the Korean War," *American Economic* Review, 87, 23-40, 1997.

Prescott, Edward. *Theory Ahead of Business Cycle Measurement*, Carnegie-Rochester Conference Series on Public Policy, 25: 11-66, 1986.

Ramsey, Frank. "A Contribution to the Theory of Taxation," *Economic Journal*, 47-61, 1927.

Rockoff, Hugh. *Drastic Measures: A History of Wage and Price Controls in the United States*. New York: Cambridge University Press, 1984.

Rogerson, Richard. "Indivisible Labor, Lotteries, and Equilibrium," *Journal of Monetary Economics*, 21: 3-16, 1988.

Sahasakul, Chaipat. "The U.S. Evidence on Optimal Taxation Over Time," *Journal of Monetary Economics*, 18: 251-275, 1986.

Seater, John. "The Market Value of Outstanding Government Debt," *Journal of Monetary Economics*, 8: 85-101, 1981.

Seater, John. "On the Construction of Marginal Federal Personal and Social Security Tax Rates in the U.S.," *Journal of Monetary Economics*, 15: 121-136, 1985.

Studenski, Paul, and Herman E. Kroos. *Financial History of the United States*. New York: McGraw-Hill, 1963.

Wynne, Mark. *Aggregate Effects of Temporary Government Purchases*. Unpublished Ph.D. Thesis. University of Rochester, Rochester, 1989.

Index

For Product Safety Concerns and Information please contact our
EU representative GPSR@taylorandfrancis.com Taylor & Francis
Verlag GmbH, Kaufingerstraße 24, 80331 München, Germany